PRAXIS 5002 Reading and Language Arts Elementary Education

By: LQ Publications

This page is intentionally left blank.

This page is intentionally left blank.

Free Online Email Tutoring Services

All preparation guides purchased directly from LQ Publications includes a free four months email tutoring subscription. Any resale of preparation guides does not qualify for a free email tutoring subscription.

What is Email Tutoring?

Email Tutoring allows buyers to send questions to tutors via email. Buyers can send any questions regarding the exam processes, strategies, content questions, or practice questions.

LQ Publications reserves the right not to answer questions with or without reason(s).

How to use Email Tutoring?

Buyers need to send an email to lqpublicationgroup@gmail.com requesting email tutoring services. Buyers may be required to confirm the email address used to purchase the preparation guide or additional information prior to using email tutoring. Once email tutoring subscription is confirmed, buyers will be provided an email address to send questions to. The four months period will start the day the subscription is confirmed.

Any misuse of email tutoring services will result in termination of services. LQ Publications reserves the right to terminate email tutoring subscription at anytime with or without notice.

Comments and Suggestions

All comments and suggestions for improvements for the study guide and email tutoring services can be sent to lqpublicationgroup@gmail.com.

This page is intentionally left blank.

Table of Content

This page is intentionally left blank.

About the Exam and Study Guide

About the PRAXIS 5002 Elementary Education English Exam

The PRAXIS 5002 Elementary Education English Exam is a test to measure individuals' knowledge related to English and reading topics introduced in Grades K-6. The exam is aligned to national standards and the Common Core State Standards, and the exam covers the following subject areas:

- Reading
- Writing
- Speaking
- Listening

The exam consists of 80 selected-response questions, and it is timed at 90 minutes. The exam questions and information are based on material typically covered in college programs related to elementary education.

What is included in this study guide book?

This guide includes two full length practice tests for the PRAXIS 5002 Elementary Education English Exam along with detail explanations to each question.

All preparation guides purchased directly from LQ Publications includes a free four months email tutoring subscription. Any resale of preparation guides does not qualify for a free email tutoring subscription.

What is Email Tutoring?

Email Tutoring allows buyers to send questions to tutors via email. Buyers can send any questions regarding the exam processes, strategies, content questions, or practice questions.

How to use Email Tutoring?

Buyers need to send an email to lqpublicationgroup@gmail.com requesting email tutoring services. Buyers may be required to confirm the email address used to purchase the preparation guide or additional information prior to using email tutoring. Once email tutoring subscription is confirmed, buyers will be provided an email address to send questions to. The four months period will start the day the subscription is confirmed.

This page is intentionally left blank.

PRACTICE EXAM 1

This page is intentionally left blank.

Answer Sheet – Exam 1

Question Numbers	Selected Answer	Question Numbers	Selected Answer	Question Numbers	Selected Answer
1		31		61	
2		32		62	
3		33		63	
4		34		64	
5		35		65	
6		36		66	
7		37		67	
8		38		68	
9		39		69	
10		40		70	
11		41		71	
12		42		72	
13		43		73	
14		44		74	
15		45		75	
16		46		76	
17		47		77	
18		48		78	
19		49		79	
20		50		80	
21		51			
22		52			
23		53			
24		54			
25		55			
26		56			
27		57			
28		58			
29		59			
30		60			

This page is intentionally left blank.

Test 1 - Full Practice Exam Questions

QUESTION 1

A teacher notices that a group of students cannot capture the big picture when reading an article related to the American Revolution. Which of the following is the best graphic organizer for helping the students understand the big picture of information text?

    A. fact pyramid

    B. story map

    C. KWL chart

    D. semantic-features analysis matrix

Answer:

QUESTION 2

Which of the following words is the best example to use when demonstrating structural analysis for vocabulary development?

    A. bike

    B. house

    C. maintain

    D. bicyclist

Answer:

QUESTION 3

A teacher requires the students to maintain a reading response journal. The primary purpose of a reading response journal is

    A. to ensure that the students are comprehending text.

    B. to support students' interaction with texts.

    C. to maintain a list of books read by the students.

    D. to ensure that the students are able to write effectively.

Answer:

QUESTION 4

Which term best describes the prewriting process?

    A. structured

    B. rigid

    C. informal

    D. careless

Answer:

QUESTION 5

Which of the following best defines the difference between decoding and encoding?

    A. Decoding refers to the process of reading – translating words into sounds and ideas. Encoding refers to building words with sounds.

    B. Encoding refers to the process of reading – translating words into sounds and ideas. Decoding refers to building words with sounds.

    C. Decoding refers to the process of writing – translating words into letters and ideas. Encoding refers to building words with sounds.

    D. Decoding refers to the process of reading – translating words into sounds and ideas. Encoding refers to building words with letters.

Answer:

QUESTION 6

I. partner students and have them listen to one another read

II. ask students to record themselves while reading

III. direct students to read the same text more than once

An elementary education teacher is looking to boost fluency. Of the above, which of the following are ways to improve fluency?

A. I and II

B. I and III

C. II and III

D. I, II, and III

Answer:

QUESTION 7

Which of the following concepts involves understanding how words are formed, and their relationship to other words in the same language?

A. morphology

B. graphophonic analysis

C. phonemic awareness

D. syntax

Answer:

QUESTION 8

A teacher is going to print cards (one set for each student) and has the students cut up the cards. Once the cards are all cut up, the students try to match the baby animal (lower case) to the mama animal (upper case) for each letter of the alphabet. The teacher is focusing on which of the following?

A. concepts of print

B. decoding

C. thinking aloud

D. alphabetic principle

Answer:

QUESTION 9

A teacher is conducting a reading comprehension lesson in which she is teaching subject/topic, main idea, and details. Which of the following options is the best example to use with the students?

A.

Subject/Topic: high blood pressure
Main Idea: Sodium can cause high blood pressure.
Detail: A lot of sodium results in water hold up that can increase pressure in the blood vessel.

B.

Main Idea: high blood pressure
Subject/Topic: Sodium can cause high blood pressure.
Detail: A lot of sodium results in water hold up that can increase pressure in the blood vessel.

C.

Subject/Topic: high blood pressure
Main Idea: A lot of sodium results in water hold up that can increase pressure in the blood vessel.
Detail: Sodium can cause high blood pressure.

D.

Subject/Topic: Sodium can cause high blood pressure high blood pressure.
Main Idea: high blood pressure
Detail: A lot of sodium results in water hold up that can increase pressure in the blood vessel.

Answer:

QUESTION 10

Megan, an elementary education teacher, has a group of students that has trouble interacting with peers during group discussions. Which of the following strategies is the best to help the students learn more appropriate oral language skills in group interactions?

A. Show students a presentation on communication skills to use in various environments.
B. Play recordings of positive group collaborations and have students analyze productive conversations.
C. While working in groups, give immediate feedback to correct oral language skills.
D. Work individually with each student struggling with oral language skills.

Answer:

QUESTION 11

Which of the following is NOT a diagraph?

A. st
B. fl
C. ch
D. wh

Answer:

QUESTION 12

Which of the following must be accomplished by the students before learning vowel diphthongs?

A. pronouns and nouns
B. spell regular words
C. spell words that rhyme
D. understand syllabication

Answer:

QUESTION 13

A fifth-grade teacher shows her students a poster that advertises orange juice. The advertisement includes multiple short statements regarding orange juice. The teacher asks the students to detect any faulty reasoning. Which of the following levels of reading comprehension is mainly being used in this activity?

A. literal
B. inferential
C. evaluative
D. appreciative

Answer:

QUESTION 14

An elementary education teacher is using an informational text regarding polar bears. When selecting vocabulary words to teach from the informational text, which of the following approaches is most beneficial?

A. selecting long words
B. selecting technical terms
C. asking students to select words
D. using experience to select words

Answer:

QUESTION 15

Which of the following assignments best assess students' use of secondary and/or primary sources?

A. Reading an article from a scientific journal regarding experiments related to birds.
B. Writing an essay on the American Revolution impact on American society.
C. Writing a personal narrative explaining how school uniform should be banned.
D. Writing a journal entry on the field trip visit to the NASA Space Center.

Answer:

QUESTION 16

The above visual can be used to teach which of the following concepts?

A. homographs
B. homophones
C. homonyms
D. synonym

Answer:

QUESTION 17

A sixth-grade student, Jimmy, who is a struggling reader, will engage in an activity in which older students read aloud predictable or rhyming books to first-grade students. This activity will most likely promote Jimmy's reading development in which of the following ways?

A. develop Jimmy's foundational reading skills
B. develop Jimmy's phonemic awareness
C. improve Jimmy's reading fluency
D. engage Jimmy in different subject topics

Answer:

QUESTION 18

An elementary teacher is conducting a lesson on fact and opinion statements. Immediately after finishing the lesson, the teacher has the students complete a worksheet on identifying fact and opinion statements. All students performed above 90% on the worksheet. Few weeks later, the teacher conducted a unit test, and all the students scored below 70% in the section assessing fact and opinion statements. Which of the instructional strategies would have been beneficial to ensure and maintain students' learning?

    A. paired activity
    B. word wall
    C. repetition
    D. reciprocal teaching

Answer:

QUESTION 19

An elementary English teacher has read an informational text regarding the Declaration of Independence to her students. The teacher wants to ensure the students have gain adequate factual information from the informational text. Which of the following would be the best to focus on?

    A. inquiry-based assessment
    B. didactic questioning
    C. at-home research project
    D. informal questionnaire assessment

Answer:

QUESTION 20

A second-grade class is learning about different fruits. The teacher asked the students to keep track of the number of apples, oranges, and pears they eat in a week for one month. The teacher wants students to create a visual to display the number of fruits eaten each week for one month. Which of the following will best display the information?

A. flow chart
B. concept map
C. bar graph
D. pi-graph

Answer:

QUESTION 21

Below is a sample sentence from a third-grade journal:

I like to eat Ice Cream as it is good but I did not get a lot last time I am going to ask my Dad to go again

Which of the following areas does the student need to show improvement in? Select THREE answers.

A. punctuation
B. capitalization
C. sentence structure
D. usage

Answer:

QUESTION 22

A sixth-grade teacher wants to support her students to become more aware of their literacy development and to better monitor development in reading. To best support this goal, the teacher should have the students

    A. compile assignments and assessments in a portfolio.
    B. complete a daily assessment record at the end of the day.
    C. set detailed goals regarding areas of improvement needed.
    D. develop rubrics to peer assess one another.

Answer:

QUESTION 23

Fourth-grade students are preparing to read a short story about two students' visit to the Boston art gallery. Which of the following activities is the best way to introduce the text to promote reading comprehension?

    A. completing a KWL chart
    B. writing about their own experience visiting an art gallery
    C. identifying Boston on a map
    D. gaining basic facts about Boston

Answer:

QUESTION 24

Which of the following sentences contains an error in punctuation?

    A. The girls went out to the store to buy fruits: apples, orange, pairs, and grapes.
    B. The baseball game was a very interesting event as many people were there
    C. I went to the shop, but I later decided to go to the movies.
    D. I really think it is time to make a change in my life; however, making a change is difficult.

Answer:

QUESTION 25

Which of the following words best describes the ending of a comedy?

    A. shocking
    B. happy
    C. sad
    D. conflict

Answer:

QUESTION 26

The following excerpt is from "The Elements of San Joaquin" (1977), a poem by Gary Soto.

At dusk the first stars appear.
Not one eager finger points toward them.
A little later the stars spread with the night
And an orange moon rises
To lead them, like a shepherd, toward dawn.

Which poetic device is used in this excerpt?

    A. idiom
    B. metaphor
    C. alliteration
    D. simile

Answer:

QUESTION 27

Which of the following sentences would be the most appropriate for an introduction to a persuasive essay?

A. Mr. Martin has been involved in all the research studies, and he is mean.
B. Doing good research with Mr. Martin looks good on your resume.
C. Mr. Martin may not be the nicest man, but he has two traits that make him a good researcher.
D. Mr. Martin has vast knowledge in research from his previous employment.

Answer:

QUESTION 28

Below is a passage from the story Pecos Bill (1966).

What Bill planned to do was leap from his horse and grab the cyclone by the neck. But as he came near and saw how high the top of the whirling tower was, he knew he would have to do something better than that. Just as he . . . came close enough to the cyclone to feel its hot breath, a knife of lightning streaked down into the ground. It struck there, quivering, just long enough for Bill to reach out and grab it. As the lightning bolt whipped back up into the sky, Bill held on. When he was as high as the top of the cyclone, he jumped and landed astraddle its black, spinning shoulders.

By then, everyone in Texas, New Mexico, Arizona, and Oklahoma was watching. They saw Bill grab hold of that cyclone's shoulders and haul them back. They saw him wrap his legs around the cyclone's belly and squeeze so hard the cyclone started to pant. Then Bill got out his lasso and slung it around the cyclone's neck. He pulled it tighter and tighter until the cyclone started to choke, spitting out rocks and dust. All the rain that was mixed up in it started to fall.

The above best represents which of the following literary genres?

A. tall tales
B. epics
C. myths
D. fairy tales

Answer:

QUESTION 29

_____ is an inclination or tendency towards an idea.

    A. Cohesion
    B. Claim
    C. Bias
    D. Push

Answer:

QUESTION 30

Below is an excerpt from "The Raven" (1845) by Edgar Allen Poe.

"Once upon a midnight dreary, while I pondered, weak and weary,
Over many a quaint and curious volume of forgotten lore,
While I nodded, nearly napping, suddenly there came a tapping,
As of some one gently rapping, rapping at my chamber door.
Tis some visitor," I muttered, "tapping at my chamber door —
Only this, and nothing more."

The repetition of similar word sounds creates a mood of

    A. cherry joy.
    B. increasing tension.
    C. growing relaxation.
    D. jubilation.

Answer:

QUESTION 31

A fifth-grade elementary teacher gives her students an article titled "Exploring Native American Culture." The teacher wants to assign a pre-reading activity that will improve students' understanding and learning while they read the article. Which of the following is the best approach to take?

    A. review technical terms
    B. discuss headings and illustrations
    C. research on Native Americans on the Internet
    D. discuss their own culture

Answer:

QUESTION 32

Read the sentence below, which contains a spelling error; then answer the question that follows.

As time passes, dietitians get better at mapping healthier eating plans that effects our health.

Which of the following words is misspelled in this sentence?

    A. dietitians
    B. mapping
    C. healthier
    D. effects

Answer:

QUESTION 33

Which of the following word identification strategies is typically the most advanced?

    A. using phonic knowledge
    B. analyzing word structure
    C. applying context clues
    D. identifying diphase vowel

Answer:

QUESTION 34

Which of the following sentences contains a relative clause?

A. That band that came to the city last month was very good at playing music.
B. After reviewing my homework, I notice I missed few problems.
C. I hated my job for years, and I wanted to quit.
D. I like to stay home, and I like to watch television.

Answer:

QUESTION 35

The following is a conversation between a teacher and her students:

Teacher: Please read this word. – Teacher will show a flashcard with the word "shop."
Students: shop
Teacher: Correct, the word is shop. Hector, how many letters are in shop?
James: S-h-o-p: four letters.
Teacher: And how many sounds are in shop, Blair?
Blair: /sh/ /o/ /p/: There are two sounds.
Teacher: How many sounds are in the word stop, Clair?
Clair: There are three sounds.
Teacher: How many sounds are in the word spin, Kate?
Kate: There are none.

Based on the conversation, which student has the least competency in blending sound?

A. James
B. Blair
C. Clair
D. Kate

Answer:

QUESTION 36

Which of the following words are appropriate to include in a lesson on the different phonemes created by r-controlled vowels?

   A. angry
   B. bird
   C. real
   D. bridge

Answer:

QUESTION 37

monolog – shipment – happily

Which of the following most accurately describes the words shown above?

   A. They contain prefixes.
   B. They are derived from German roots.
   C. They have multiple meanings.
   D. They contain suffixes.

Answer:

QUESTION 38

He will have arrived.

The above sentence reflects which verb tense?

   A. future
   B. present
   C. future perfect
   D. present perfect

Answer:

QUESTION 39

- writes uppercase and lowercase letters
- writes own name
- uses invented spellings to express meaning
- uses invented spellings to write teacher-dictated words

The above skills are achieved at what grade level?

A. Pre-K
B. Kindergarten
C. First
D. Second

Answer:

QUESTION 40

Because the chicken was too cold, I warmed it in the microwave.

The above is an example of which type of sentence?

A. run-on
B. compound
C. complex
D. compound-complex

Answer:

QUESTION 41

A sixth-grade teacher writes the following on the board:

work

n. a task or tasks to be undertaken

v. operate or function

Which of the following sentences uses "work" as a noun, as in the first definition given?

A. He works at the office on the other side of town.
B. You need to go back to work.
C. His work was not that bad.
D. Jane is going to work at the office starting next week.

Answer:

QUESTION 42

The following is a selection from Alfred Noyes' poem "The Highwayman."

The wind was a torrent of darkness among the gusty trees.
The moon was a ghostly galleon tossed upon cloudy seas.
The road was a ribbon of moonlight over the purple moor,
And the highwayman came riding—
Riding—riding—
The highwayman came riding, up to the old inn-door.

He'd a French cocked-hat on his forehead, a bunch of lace at his chin,
A coat of the claret velvet, and breeches of brown doe-skin.
They fitted with never a wrinkle. His boots were up to the thigh.
And he rode with a jewelled twinkle,
His pistol butts a-twinkle,
His rapier hilt a-twinkle, under the jewelled sky.

The poem starts off with which of the following literary elements?

    A. metaphor
    B. personification
    C. oxymoron
    D. hyperbole

Answer:

QUESTION 43

in front – behind – near – over

The above words are linked to which organization of writing?

    A. chronological sequence
    B. spatial sequence
    C. cause and effect
    D. problem and solution

Answer:

QUESTION 44

A teacher is looking to introduce the different types of genres to a class in order to compare and contrast information about a subject. Which of the following instructional strategies is the most effective?

A. read aloud
B. book clubs
C. choral reading
D. text sets

Answer:

QUESTION 45

A sixth-grade class assignment involves deciding which country to plan a vacation with family members. The best resource for the students to use would be a(an)

A. encyclopedia.
B. dictionary.
C. periodical.
D. atlas.

Answer:

QUESTION 46

Which of the following best describes a student at the transitional stage of writing development?

A. Letters are written to represent some of the sounds in words.
B. Letters are written to represent most sounds in words.
C. Letters are written according to common spelling patterns and include silent letters.
D. Letters are written to represent words.

Answer:

QUESTION 47

Which of the following would be the most critical to include in an introduction for a persuasive essay?

A. counterargument
B. quotes
C. importance of issue addressed
D. details about the author

Answer:

QUESTION 48

In which of the following sentences is the underlined word incorrectly used?

A. It is not _me_ you should blame.
B. She and _I_ always get along but not last week.
C. The girls and _I_ want to leave school early to go to the movies.
D. When will _I_ get my coffee cup back?

Answer:

QUESTION 49

Which of the following functional texts would NOT be effective for spelling words related to cooking?

A. an encyclopedia
B. a thesaurus
C. a dictionary
D. an atlas

Answer:

QUESTION 50

Which of the following describes a set of conventions for writing a language?

    A. pragmatics
    B. phonetics
    C. orthography
    D. morphology

Answer:

QUESTION 51

Which of the following aspects of literacy is important to early and continuous reading development for elementary-level reading curriculum?

    A. vocabulary
    B. context clue
    C. concept of print
    D. exposure to children's literature

Answer:

QUESTION 52

A third-grade teacher is planning to use flexible grouping to differentiate reading instruction. When arranging students in small groups, the key aspect for the teacher to consider first is which of the following?

    A. individual strengths
    B. individual interests
    C. specific writing skill goals
    D. specific writing skill needs

Answer:

QUESTION 53

In an explicit instruction lesson, teachers provide modeling, scaffolding, and prompting until students are able to apply a skill independently. The guided practice phases includes:

I.   modeling
II. guided practice
III. unprompted practice

The following actions are being undertaken by a teacher:

- Demonstrate the skill or strategy.
- Use "think alouds" to describe how to apply the skill or strategy.
- Use clear, consistent, and direct language.

Which of the following guided practice phases are displayed by the teacher's action?

A. I only
B. II only
C. I and II
D. I and III

Answer:

QUESTION 54

A fourth-grade student who is reading independently has difficulty decoding the word "deescalate." Which of the following decoding strategies would most likely assist the student in identifying the word?

A. applying phonic knowledge
B. using structural analysis
C. recognizing patterns
D. using thesaurus

Answer:

QUESTION 55

A third-grade teacher is planning a lesson focused on decoding multisyllabic words that contain common prefixes. Which of the following word lists would be most appropriate to include in this lesson?

    A. cake, bake, make
    B. rerun, review, unable, unseen
    C. sun, bun, fun
    D. undo, unknown, unappreciative

Answer:

QUESTION 56

A fourth-grade teacher is going to read a short informational text regarding rocket science. After reading to the whole class, the teacher will pair students to read the same text to each other. Which of the following planned support is NOT used?

    A. modeling
    B. repetition
    C. summarizing
    D. paired activity

Answer:

QUESTION 57

A fifth-grade teacher includes instruction in word learning strategies as one component in an interdisciplinary approach to vocabulary development. For example, after the students start reading about plants in a science textbook, the teacher conducts a lesson focused on assisting students learn the concepts and vocabulary introduced in the text. Which of the following word-learning strategies would best develop students' vocabulary?

    A. learning a semantic feature analysis
    B. using flashcards to learn words
    C. reading articles on new words
    D. finding facts related to vocabulary words

Answer:

QUESTION 58

A sixth-grade teacher writes the words cunning, cumbersome, and astonishing on the Smart Board, and she provides a definition for each of the words. Which of the following steps would be most effective for the teacher to take next to deepen the students' knowledge of the words?

- A. having the students repeat the definition
- B. showing flashcards and having the students define words
- C. having the students write sentences using the words
- D. providing examples showing the right and the wrong way of using each word

Answer:

QUESTION 59

Students in a sixth-grade class read a lengthy newspaper article regarding the importance of uniform policies in schools. After a class discussion of the author's points, the teacher begins a lesson discussing the pros and cons of uniforms in school settings. Which of the following types of graphic organizers would be most effective to use in this lesson?

- A. a flowchart
- B. an outline
- C. a T-chart
- D. a Venn-diagram

Answer:

QUESTION 60

Use the poem below by William Shakespeare to answer the question.

"When well-appareled April on the heel
Of limping winter treads."

Which of the following poetic devices is used most prominently in the poem?

    A. personification
    B. hyperbole
    C. simile
    D. ambiguity

Answer:

QUESTION 61

Which of the following sets of words is most closely associated with if/then text structure?

    A. since, result, consequently
    B. while, yet, similarly
    C. in addition, moreover, additionally
    D. such as, by, more

Answer:

QUESTION 62

Knowledge of the relationship between letters and sounds is _____.

    A. phonemic awareness
    B. fluency
    C. vocabulary
    D. phonics

Answer:

QUESTION 63

A first-grade teacher is spending a portion of the afternoon having students write and draw in personal journals. The students are free to write and draw about any topic they desire. This approach will mainly benefit students by promoting their ability to

A. think creatively.
B. think deeply.
C. get personal.
D. improve grammar.

Answer:

QUESTION 64

Which of the following is NOT one of the five essential components of reading identified by the National Reading Panel?

A. phonics
B. fluency
C. vocabulary
D. spelling

Answer:

QUESTION 65

Understanding social and emotional aspects is linked mostly to which levels of reading comprehension?

A. lexical comprehension
B. literal comprehension
C. interpretive comprehension
D. affective comprehension

Answer:

QUESTION 66

Which of the following is NOT an open syllable word?

A. no
B. my
C. fly
D. hat

Answer:

QUESTION 67

Which of the following is most accurate regarding fiction and nonfiction text?

A. Fiction can be both narrative and informational.
B. Nonfiction can be both narrative and informational.
C. Fiction can be informational only.
D. Nonfiction can be informational only.

Answer:

QUESTION 68

An elementary teacher has her students read the story "The Mitten." Then, she gives her students a worksheet with images of different animals, and she instructs her students to label the animals below in the order they were introduced in the story. Which of the following reading strategies is being most targeted in this activity?

A. recalling
B. retelling
C. sequencing
D. summarizing

Answer:

QUESTION 69

An elementary reading teacher is looking to get her students involved in self-assessing their own reading skills. Which of the following is the best activity to accomplish this goal?

A. choral reading
B. taped reading
C. echo reading
D. buddy reading

Answer:

QUESTION 70

Which of the following is NOT written in the first person?

A. autobiography
B. memoir
C. personal essay
D. biography

Answer:

QUESTION 71

Which of the following is NOT a consonant blend?

A. bl
B. br
C. ar
D. spl

Answer:

QUESTION 72

Since the weather is bad, I'll stay inside for the remainder of the night.

The above sentence is which of the following?

A. simple sentence
B. complex sentence
C. compound sentence
D. compound-complex sentence

Answer:

QUESTION 73

In early elementary grade levels, which of the following methods is important for improving a student's reading fluency?

A. Giving the student easy reading passages to read.
B. Giving the student multiple opportunities to reread the same passages.
C. Teaching the student vocabulary words prior to reading the passages.
D. Providing the student with a summary of the reading passages.

Answer:

QUESTION 74

Some people love cold winters near the fireplace with hot coffee. Others love the hot summer with snow cones and ice cream cones. Write an essay that names your favorite season and give reasons why it is best.

The above prompt is associated with which type of writing?

A. narrative
B. descriptive
C. expository
D. persuasive

Answer:

QUESTION 75

Below is a sample work from a sixth-grade student:

There are many sales going on during the Black Friday Holiday Sales. There are stores that provide many discounts on electronics and clothing. There can be stores that even offer free stuff during the holiday season. There can be so much fun during the holiday period.

Which is NOT an area the student needs improvement in?

A. word choice
B. capitalization
C. sentence structure
D. spelling

Answer:

QUESTION 76

Jack is having some difficulty in reading as indicated by his score on an oral reading fluency assessment. When he reads, he sometimes inserts words that are not in the text. This shows a weakness in which area of fluency?

A. prosody
B. rate
C. accuracy
D. automaticity

Answer:

QUESTION 77

More than 70% of a first-grade class scored at high risk on the oral reading fluency assessment. Which instructional practice would be most effective for improving the students' oral reading fluency?

    A. daily independent reading in the afternoon
    B. peer reading on familiar text
    C. vocabulary development on unfamiliar words
    D. constantly reading text with corrective feedback

Answer:

QUESTION 78

While reading a book aloud, one of the students believes the teacher is reading the pictures instead of the words in the book. Which of the following is the student lacking in understanding?

    A. letter movement
    B. phonological awareness
    C. concepts of print
    D. alphabetic principle

Answer:

QUESTION 79

A teacher asks her kindergarten students to say words sound by sound while moving balls for each sound. This approach is showing what instructional method?

    A. intensive instruction
    B. explicit systematic instruction
    C. differentiated instruction
    D. shared reading

Answer:

QUESTION 80

A fifth-grade teacher models how to select unknown words and write explanations, reread areas where they struggle to understand, write questions based on the passages, and infer what will happen in the next passage.

These are examples of comprehension strategies that include:

    A. clarifying, summarizing, questioning, and predicting
    B. clarifying, monitoring, questioning, and predicting
    C. defining, monitoring, previewing, and predicting
    D. clarifying, monitoring, questioning, and previewing

Answer:

This page is intentionally left blank.

Answer Key – Exam 1

Question Numbers	Correct Answer	Question Numbers	Correct Answer	Question Numbers	Correct Answer
1	A	31	B	61	A
2	D	32	D	62	D
3	B	33	B	63	A
4	C	34	A	64	D
5	A	35	D	65	D
6	D	36	B	66	D
7	A	37	D	67	B
8	D	38	C	68	C
9	A	39	B	69	B
10	B	40	C	70	D
11	B	41	C	71	C
12	B	42	A	72	B
13	C	43	B	73	B
14	C	44	B	74	D
15	B	45	D	75	D
16	A	46	C	76	A
17	C	47	C	77	D
18	C	48	A	78	C
19	B	49	D	79	B
20	C	50	C	80	B
21	A,B, and C	51	A		
22	C	52	D		
23	A	53	A		
24	B	54	B		
25	B	55	B		
26	D	56	C		
27	C	57	A		
28	A	58	D		
29	C	59	C		
30	B	60	A		

NOTE: Getting approximately 80% of the questions correct increases chances of obtaining passing score on the real exam. This varies from different states and university programs.

This page is intentionally left blank.

Test 1 - Full Practice Exam Questions and Explanations

QUESTION 1

A teacher notices that a group of students cannot capture the big picture when reading an article related to the American Revolution. Which of the following is the best graphic organizer for helping the students understand the big picture of information text?

- A. fact pyramid
- B. story map
- C. KWL chart
- D. semantic-features analysis matrix

Answer: A

Explanation: Fact pyramids provide teachers with a structured way of analyzing information in textbooks to guide students' focus toward big ideas. Fact pyramid graphically categorizes text information into three levels: (1) essential facts ;(2) short-term facts; and (3) supportive detail.

QUESTION 2

Which of the following words is the best example to use when demonstrating structural analysis for vocabulary development?

- A. bike
- B. house
- C. maintain
- D. bicyclist

Answer: D

Explanation: Structural analysis involves using prefixes, suffixes, and root words to determine the meaning of an unfamiliar word. The word "bicyclist" is the only word that has a prefix, suffix, and root word, so it would be the best and the most useful in teaching structural analysis. The keyword in the question is "best," so the key is to select a word that involves structural analysis the most.

QUESTION 3

A teacher requires the students to maintain a reading response journal. The primary purpose of a reading response journal is

A. to ensure that the students are comprehending text.
B. to support students' interaction with texts.
C. to maintain a list of books read by the students.
D. to ensure that the students are able to write effectively.

Answer: B

Explanation: Reading response journal is a place for students to write, draw, and share their opinions, ideas, or responses to text read in the class. The purpose of a reading response journal is to support students' interaction with texts.

QUESTION 4

Which term best describes the prewriting process?

A. structured
B. rigid
C. informal
D. careless

Answer: C

Explanation: Prewriting stage includes discussing notes and jotting down notes, which is best linked to the word informal.

QUESTION 5

Which of the following best defines the difference between decoding and encoding?

    A. Decoding refers to the process of reading – translating words into sounds and ideas. Encoding refers to building words with sounds.

    B. Encoding refers to the process of reading – translating words into sounds and ideas. Decoding refers to building words with sounds.

    C. Decoding refers to the process of writing – translating words into letters and ideas. Encoding refers to building words with sounds.

    D. Decoding refers to the process of reading – translating words into sounds and ideas. Encoding refers to building words with letters.

Answer: A

Explanation: Decoding refers to the process of reading – translating words into sounds and ideas. Encoding refers to building words with sounds.

QUESTION 6

    I. partner students and have them listen to one another read

    II. ask students to record themselves while reading

    III. direct students to read the same text more than once

An elementary education teacher is looking to boost fluency. Of the above, which of the following are ways to improve fluency?

    A. I and II

    B. I and III

    C. II and III

    D. I, II, and III

Answer: D

Explanation: Fluency is defined as the ability to read with speed, accuracy, and proper expression. All options are ways to improve fluency.

QUESTION 7

Which of the following concepts involves understanding how words are formed, and their relationship to other words in the same language?

    A. morphology
    B. graphophonic analysis
    C. phonemic awareness
    D. syntax

Answer: A

Explanation: Morphology is the study of the internal construction of words. In particular, morphology is how words are formed and their relationship to other words in the same language.

QUESTION 8

A teacher is going to print cards (one set for each student) and has the students cut up the cards. Once the cards are all cut up, the students try to match the baby animal (lower case) to the mama animal (upper case) for each letter of the alphabet. The teacher is focusing on which of the following?

    A. concepts of print
    B. decoding
    C. thinking aloud
    D. alphabetic principle

Answer: D

Explanation: The information gained from this activity is helpful in knowing where a student is with understanding alphabetic principle, which is the understanding that there are systematic and predictable relationships between spoken sounds and written letters.

QUESTION 9

A teacher is conducting a reading comprehension lesson in which she is teaching subject/topic, main idea, and details. Which of the following options is the best example to use with the students?

A.

Subject/Topic: high blood pressure
Main Idea: Sodium can cause high blood pressure.
Detail: A lot of sodium results in water hold up that can increase pressure in the blood vessel.

B.

Main Idea: high blood pressure
Subject/Topic: Sodium can cause high blood pressure.
Detail: A lot of sodium results in water hold up that can increase pressure in the blood vessel.

C.

Subject/Topic: high blood pressure
Main Idea: A lot of sodium results in water hold up that can increase pressure in the blood vessel.
Detail: Sodium can cause high blood pressure.

D.

Subject/Topic: Sodium can cause high blood pressure high blood pressure.
Main Idea: high blood pressure
Detail: A lot of sodium results in water hold up that can increase pressure in the blood vessel.

Answer: A

Explanation: The main topic is related to high blood pressure while the main idea is concerning sodium causing high blood pressure. The detail in Option A is appropriate for the topic and main idea.

QUESTION 10

Megan, an elementary education teacher, has a group of students that has trouble interacting with peers during group discussions. Which of the following strategies is the best to help the students learn more appropriate oral language skills in group interactions?

    A. Show students a presentation on communication skills to use in various environments.
    B. Play recordings of positive group collaborations and have students analyze productive conversations.
    C. While working in groups, give immediate feedback to correct oral language skills.
    D. Work individually with each student struggling with oral language skills.

Answer: B

Explanation: Getting students exposed to appropriate group interactions is a good strategy to employ. Moreover, the students are going to analyze the conversations, which they can recall during future group discussions.

QUESTION 11

Which of the following is NOT a diagraph?

    A. st
    B. fl
    C. ch
    D. wh

Answer: B

Explanation: Diagraphs are "voiceless" combinations of two consonants. Option B is a consonant blend.

QUESTION 12

Which of the following must be accomplished by the students before learning vowel diphthongs?

    A. pronouns and nouns
    B. spell regular words
    C. spell words that rhyme
    D. understand syllabication

Answer: B

Explanation: Vowel diphthongs are characteristic of irregularly spelled words, so students must learn to spell regular words before going into vowel diphthongs.

QUESTION 13

A fifth-grade teacher shows her students a poster that advertises orange juice. The advertisement includes multiple short statements regarding orange juice. The teacher asks the students to detect any faulty reasoning. Which of the following levels of reading comprehension is mainly being used in this activity?

    A. literal
    B. inferential
    C. evaluative
    D. appreciative

Answer: C

Explanation: The students evaluate statements of orange juice to their own experience and knowledge, so the skill used in the activity is evaluative.

QUESTION 14

An elementary education teacher is using an informational text regarding polar bears. When selecting vocabulary words to teach from the informational text, which of the following approaches is most beneficial?

    A. selecting long words
    B. selecting technical terms
    C. asking students to select words
    D. using experience to select words

Answer: C

Explanation: Having students select words to further study will be targeted towards their needs. Of the options provided, Option C is the best one that is most beneficial to the students.

QUESTION 15

Which of the following assignments best assess students' use of secondary and/or primary sources?

    A. Reading an article from a scientific journal regarding experiments related to birds.
    B. Writing an essay on the American Revolution's impact on American society.
    C. Writing a personal narrative explaining how school uniforms should be banned.
    D. Writing a journal entry on the field trip visit to the NASA Space Center.

Answer: B

Explanation: Option B is the only option that directly requires the use of secondary and/or primary sources.

QUESTION 16

The above visual can be used to teach which of the following concepts?

    A. homographs
    B. homophones
    C. homonyms
    D. synonym

Answer: A

Explanation: A homograph is a word that has the same spelling as another word but has a different sound and a different meaning. The word wind is a homograph.

QUESTION 17

A sixth-grade student, Jimmy, who is a struggling reader, will engage in an activity in which older students read aloud predictable or rhyming books to first-grade students. This activity will most likely promote Jimmy's reading development in which of the following ways?

    A. develop Jimmy's foundational reading skills
    B. develop Jimmy's phonemic awareness
    C. improve Jimmy's reading fluency
    D. engage Jimmy in different subject topics

Answer: C

Explanation: The key in the question is "predictable or rhyming" books, which contain multiple repetition of words and phrases. This allows the student to develop automaticity, accuracy, and prosody (appropriate expression), which are reading fluency skills.

QUESTION 18

An elementary teacher is conducting a lesson on fact and opinion statements. Immediately after finishing the lesson, the teacher has the students complete a worksheet on identifying fact and opinion statements. All students performed above 90% on the worksheet. Few weeks later, the teacher conducted a unit test, and all the students scored below 70% in the section assessing fact and opinion statements. Which of the instructional strategies would have been beneficial to ensure and maintain students' learning?

    A. paired activity
    B. word wall
    C. repetition
    D. reciprocal teaching

Answer: C

Explanation: Repetition of the activity will have allowed the students to engage more regarding fact and opinion statements, which would increase the chances of maintaining knowledge. This can support the students in continuously doing well on assessments.

QUESTION 19

An elementary English teacher has read an informational text regarding the Declaration of Independence to her students. The teacher wants to ensure the students have gain adequate factual information from the informational text. Which of the following would be the best to focus on?

    A. inquiry-based assessment
    B. didactic questioning
    C. at-home research project
    D. informal questionnaire assessment

Answer: B

Explanation: Didactic questioning focuses on factual questions and not open-ended questions. Since the reading is related to social studies, which contain a lot of facts, using didactic questions is the best approach.

QUESTION 20

A second-grade class is learning about different fruits. The teacher asked the students to keep track of the number of apples, oranges, and pears they eat in a week for one month. The teacher wants students to create a visual to display the number of fruits eaten each week for one month. Which of the following will best display the information?

    A. flow chart
    B. concept map
    C. bar graph
    D. pi-graph

Answer: C

Explanation: A bar graph can show how many fruits were eaten each week. The other options are not appropriate for displaying the information presented in the questions.

QUESTION 21

Below is a sample sentence from a third-grade journal:

I like to eat Ice Cream as it is good but I did not get a lot last time I am going to ask my Dad to go again

Which of the following areas does the student need to show improvement in? Select THREE answers.

    A. punctuation
    B. capitalization
    C. sentence structure
    D. usage

Answer: A, B, and C

Explanation: The student did not use any punctuation in the sentence. The student capitalized "Ice Cream" and "Dad" unnecessarily. The sentence is a run-on sentence, so the structure needs to be fixed.

QUESTION 22

A sixth-grade teacher wants to support her students to become more aware of their literacy development and to better monitor development in reading. To best support this goal, the teacher should have the students

    A. compile assignments and assessments in a portfolio.
    B. complete a daily assessment record at the end of the day.
    C. set detailed goals regarding areas of improvement needed.
    D. develop rubrics to peer assess one another.

Answer: C

Explanation: Having students set goals for improvement areas supports the idea of getting them involved in monitoring skills related to reading.

QUESTION 23

Fourth-grade students are preparing to read a short story about two students' visit to the Boston art gallery. Which of the following activities is the best way to introduce the text to promote reading comprehension?

    A. completing a KWL chart
    B. writing about their own experience visiting an art gallery
    C. identifying Boston on a map
    D. gaining basic facts about Boston

Answer: A

Explanation: KWL charts allow the students to document what they know before reading and after reading, which allows students to build knowledge and support reading comprehension.

QUESTION 24

Which of the following sentences contains an error in punctuation?

    A. The girls went out to the store to buy fruits: apples, orange, pairs, and grapes.
    B. The baseball game was a very interesting event as many people were there
    C. I went to the shop, but I later decided to go to the movies.
    D. I really think it is time to make a change in my life; however, making a change is difficult.

Answer: B

Explanation: A period is needed at the end of the sentence in Option B.

QUESTION 25

Which of the following words best describes the ending of a comedy?

    A. shocking
    B. happy
    C. sad
    D. conflict

Answer: B

Explanation: A comedy is to assume or delight the audience, and the action in a comedy usually ends happily.

QUESTION 26

The following excerpt is from "The Elements of San Joaquin" (1977), a poem by Gary Soto.

At dusk the first stars appear.
Not one eager finger points toward them.
A little later the stars spread with the night
And an orange moon rises
To lead them, like a shepherd, toward dawn.

Which poetic device is used in this excerpt?

    A. idiom
    B. metaphor
    C. alliteration
    D. simile

Answer: D

Explanation: In the last two lines of the excerpt, a simile is used to compare the moon to a shepherd. Simile is a figure of speech involving the comparison of one thing with another thing of a different kind.

QUESTION 27

Which of the following sentences would be the most appropriate for an introduction to a persuasive essay?

    A. Mr. Martin has been involved in all the research studies, and he is mean.
    B. Doing good research with Mr. Martin looks good on your resume.
    C. Mr. Martin may not be the nicest man, but he has two traits that make him a good researcher.
    D. Mr. Martin has vast knowledge in research from his previous employment.

Answer: C

Explanation: Option C provides a clear and concise sentence that gives an overview of what will be discussed in the writing piece. The sentence clearly sets the stage about how Mr. Martin is nice and has traits that make him a good researcher.

QUESTION 28

Below is a passage from the story Pecos Bill (1966).

What Bill planned to do was leap from his horse and grab the cyclone by the neck. But as he came near and saw how high the top of the whirling tower was, he knew he would have to do something better than that. Just as he . . . came close enough to the cyclone to feel its hot breath, a knife of lightning streaked down into the ground. It struck there, quivering, just long enough for Bill to reach out and grab it. As the lightning bolt whipped back up into the sky, Bill held on. When he was as high as the top of the cyclone, he jumped and landed astraddle its black, spinning shoulders.

By then, everyone in Texas, New Mexico, Arizona, and Oklahoma was watching. They saw Bill grab hold of that cyclone's shoulders and haul them back. They saw him wrap his legs around the cyclone's belly and squeeze so hard the cyclone started to pant. Then Bill got out his lasso and slung it around the cyclone's neck. He pulled it tighter and tighter until the cyclone started to choke, spitting out rocks and dust. All the rain that was mixed up in it started to fall.

The above best represents which of the following literary genres?

  A. tall tales
  B. epics
  C. myths
  D. fairy tales

Answer: A

Explanation: A tall tale is a story with unbelievable and highly improbable elements, related as if it were true and factual.

QUESTION 29

_____ is an inclination or tendency towards an idea.

    A. Cohesion
    B. Claim
    C. Bias
    D. Push

Answer: C

Explanation: Cohesion is the flow of sentences, paragraphs, or sections of text to show connection among ideas. Claim is an arguable statement. Bias is an inclination or tendency towards an idea.

QUESTION 30

Below is an excerpt from "The Raven" (1845) by Edgar Allen Poe.

"Once upon a midnight dreary, while I pondered, weak and weary,
Over many a quaint and curious volume of forgotten lore,
While I nodded, nearly napping, suddenly there came a tapping,
As of some one gently rapping, rapping at my chamber door.
Tis some visitor," I muttered, "tapping at my chamber door —
Only this, and nothing more."

The repetition of similar word sounds creates a mood of

    A. cherry joy.
    B. increasing tension.
    C. growing relaxation.
    D. jubilation.

Answer: B

Explanation: Poe continuously repeats the sounds (e.g. "-apping") to create a sense of urgency and increasing tension.

QUESTION 31

A fifth-grade elementary teacher gives her students an article titled "Exploring Native American Culture." The teacher wants to assign a pre-reading activity that will improve students' understanding and learning while they read the article. Which of the following is the best approach to take?

    A. review technical terms
    B. discuss headings and illustrations
    C. research on Native Americans on the Internet
    D. discuss their own culture

Answer: B

Explanation: Discussing headings and illustrations will allow the students to get a sense of what they will read, which can support them in understanding and learning while they read the article.

QUESTION 32

Read the sentence below, which contains a spelling error; then answer the question that follows.

As time passes, dietitians get better at mapping healthier eating plans that effects our health.

Which of the following words is misspelled in this sentence?

    A. dietitians
    B. mapping
    C. healthier
    D. effects

Answer: D

Explanation: The correct spelling is "affects."

QUESTION 33

Which of the following word identification strategies is typically the most advanced?

    A. using phonic knowledge
    B. analyzing word structure
    C. applying context clues
    D. identifying diphase vowel

Answer: B

Explanation: The most advanced word identification strategy is analyzing word structure. Analyzing involves using critical thinking skills.

QUESTION 34

Which of the following sentences contains a relative clause?

    A. That band that came to the city last month was very good at playing music.
    B. After reviewing my homework, I notice I missed few problems.
    C. I hated my job for years, and I wanted to quit.
    D. I like to stay home, and I like to watch television.

Answer: A

Explanation: Relative clauses are clauses starting with the relative pronouns who, that, which, whose, where, when.

QUESTION 35

The following is a conversation between a teacher and her students:

Teacher: Please read this word. – Teacher will show a flashcard with the word "shop."
Students: shop
Teacher: Correct, the word is shop. Hector, how many letters are in shop?
James: S-h-o-p: four letters.
Teacher: And how many sounds are in shop, Blair?
Blair: /sh/ /o/ /p/: There are two sounds.
Teacher: How many sounds are in the word stop, Clair?
Clair: There are three sounds.
Teacher: How many sounds are in the word spin, Kate?
Kate: There are none.

Based on the conversation, which student has the least competency in blending sound?

A. James
B. Blair
C. Clair
D. Kate

Answer: D

Explanation: Kate indicates that there are no sounds in the word "spin." This is a clear indication that her skills related to blending sound is the lowest.

QUESTION 36

Which of the following words are appropriate to include in a lesson on the different phonemes created by r-controlled vowels?

    A. angry
    B. bird
    C. real
    D. bridge

Answer: B

Explanation: The /ir/ sound in "bird" is an r-controlled sound.

QUESTION 37

monolog – shipment – happily

Which of the following most accurately describes the words shown above?

    A. They contain prefixes.
    B. They are derived from German roots.
    C. They have multiple meanings.
    D. They contain suffixes.

Answer: D

Explanation: Each of the words have a suffix. Monolog has "log." Shipment has "ment." Happily has "ly."

QUESTION 38

He will have arrived.

The above sentence reflects which verb tense?

A. future
B. present
C. future perfect
D. present perfect

Answer: C

Explanation: Future perfect is when an action will have been completed at some point in the future. The present perfect tense refers to an action or state that either occurred at an indefinite time in the past or began in the past and continued to the present time.

QUESTION 39

- writes uppercase and lowercase letters
- writes own name
- uses invented spellings to express meaning
- uses invented spellings to write teacher-dictated words

The above skills are achieved at what grade level?

A. Pre-K
B. Kindergarten
C. First
D. Second

Answer: B

Explanation: The skills outlined indicate achievement at the kindergarten level.

QUESTION 40

Because the chicken was too cold, I warmed it in the microwave.

The above is an example of which type of sentence?

    A. run-on

    B. compound

    C. complex

    D. compound-complex

Answer: C

Explanation: A complex sentence combines a dependent clause with an independent clause. When the dependent clause is placed before the independent clause, the two clauses are divided by a comma; otherwise, no punctuation is needed.

QUESTION 41

A sixth-grade teacher writes the following on the board:

    work

    n. a task or tasks to be undertaken

    v. operate or function

Which of the following sentences uses "work" as a noun, as in the first definition given?

    A. He works at the office on the other side of town.

    B. You need to go back to work.

    C. His work was not that bad.

    D. Jane is going to work at the office starting next week.

Answer: C

Explanation: The word "work" is used as a noun in Option C. Option A, B, and D uses "work" as a verb.

QUESTION 42

The following is a selection from Alfred Noyes' poem "The Highwayman."

The wind was a torrent of darkness among the gusty trees.
The moon was a ghostly galleon tossed upon cloudy seas.
The road was a ribbon of moonlight over the purple moor,
And the highwayman came riding—
Riding—riding—
The highwayman came riding, up to the old inn-door.

He'd a French cocked-hat on his forehead, a bunch of lace at his chin,
A coat of the claret velvet, and breeches of brown doe-skin.
They fitted with never a wrinkle. His boots were up to the thigh.
And he rode with a jewelled twinkle,
His pistol butts a-twinkle,
His rapier hilt a-twinkle, under the jewelled sky.

The poem starts off with which of the following literary elements?

    A. metaphor
    B. personification
    C. oxymoron
    D. hyperbole

Answer: A

Explanation: The poem starts off with wind being called "torrent of darkness," which is an intense image establishing a feeling of violence and chaotic feeling. Metaphor is a figure of speech in which a word or phrase is applied to an object or action to which it is not literally applicable.

QUESTION 43

in front – behind – near – over

The above words are linked to which organization of writing?

    A. chronological sequence

    B. spatial sequence

    C. cause and effect

    D. problem and solution

Answer: B

Explanation: All the words relate to space, so the organization of writing is spatial sequence.

QUESTION 44

A teacher is looking to introduce the different types of genres to a class in order to compare and contrast information about a subject. Which of the following instructional strategies is the most effective?

    A. read aloud

    B. book clubs

    C. choral reading

    D. text sets

Answer: B

Explanation: Book clubs typically keep things interesting by changing genres, so the teacher can introduce the concept of book clubs.

QUESTION 45

A sixth-grade class assignment involves deciding which country to plan a vacation with family members. The best resource for the students to use would be a(an)

A. encyclopedia.
B. dictionary.
C. periodical.
D. atlas.

Answer: D

Explanation: Atlas includes maps of different regions, which can support students in deciding which country to go for vacation.

QUESTION 46

Which of the following best describes a student at the transitional stage of writing development?

A. Letters are written to represent some of the sounds in words.
B. Letters are written to represent most sounds in words.
C. Letters are written according to common spelling patterns and include silent letters.
D. Letters are written to represent words.

Answer: C

Explanation: Transitional stage of writing display the ability to create meaningful sentences to communicate a message. This includes writing letters according to common spelling patterns.

QUESTION 47

Which of the following would be the most critical to include in an introduction for a persuasive essay?

A. counterargument
B. quotes
C. importance of issue addressed
D. details about the author

Answer: C

Explanation: Quotes, counterarguments, and details about the author are not necessary in a persuasive essay. However, discussing the importance of the issue is an important part of an introduction to a persuasive essay.

QUESTION 48

In which of the following sentences is the underlined word incorrectly used?

A. It is not <u>me</u> you should blame.
B. She and <u>I</u> always get along but not last week.
C. The girls and <u>I</u> want to leave school early to go to the movies.
D. When will <u>I</u> get my coffee cup back?

Answer: A

Explanation: "I" is a nominative pronoun, which means that it is used as the subject of a sentence, or as a predicate nominative. The correct word to use is "I."

QUESTION 49

Which of the following functional texts would NOT be effective for spelling words related to cooking?

   A. an encyclopedia
   B. a thesaurus
   C. a dictionary
   D. an atlas

Answer: D

Explanation: An atlas is a collection of maps, which will not consist of words related to cooking. There are encyclopedias related to cooking that can help individuals with spelling. A thesaurus and a dictionary can support individuals in spelling.

QUESTION 50

Which of the following describes a set of conventions for writing a language?

   A. pragmatics
   B. phonetics
   C. orthography
   D. morphology

Answer: C

Explanation: Orthography is a set of conventions for writing a language.

QUESTION 51

Which of the following aspects of literacy is important to early and continuous reading development for elementary-level reading curriculum?

    A. vocabulary
    B. context clue
    C. concept of print
    D. exposure to children's literature

Answer: A

Explanation: Getting exposed to as many vocabulary words will help in reading comprehension. In addition, vocabulary development supports the development of phonological awareness and decoding skills.

QUESTION 52

A third-grade teacher is planning to use flexible grouping to differentiate reading instruction. When arranging students in small groups, the key aspect for the teacher to consider first is which of the following?

    A. individual strengths
    B. individual interests
    C. specific writing skill goals
    D. specific writing skill needs

Answer: D

Explanation: Flexible grouping is a term that covers a range of grouping students for delivering instruction, such as whole class, small group, and partner. Grouping students that need help in the same area will allow the teacher to provide targeted and focused instruction.

QUESTION 53

In an explicit instruction lesson, teachers provide modeling, scaffolding, and prompting until the students are able to apply a skill independently. The guided practice phases include:

    I.   modeling
    II.   guided practice
   III. unprompted practice

The following actions are being undertaken by a teacher:

- Demonstrate the skill or strategy.
- Use "think alouds" to describe how to apply the skill or strategy.
- Use clear, consistent, and direct language.

Which of the following guided practice phases are displayed by the teacher's action?

A. I only
B. II only
C. I and II
D. I and III

Answer: A

Explanation: Modeling involves the teacher doing most of the action, which is displayed in the list.

QUESTION 54

A fourth-grade student who is reading independently has difficulty decoding the word "deescalate." Which of the following decoding strategies would most likely assist the student in identifying the word?

    A. applying phonic knowledge
    B. using structural analysis
    C. recognizing patterns
    D. using thesaurus

Answer: B

Explanation: Structure analysis is the process of dividing words into morphemes.

QUESTION 55

A third-grade teacher is planning a lesson focused on decoding multisyllabic words that contain common prefixes. Which of the following word lists would be most appropriate to include in this lesson?

    A. cake, bake, make
    B. rerun, review, unable, unseen
    C. sun, bun, fun
    D. undo, unknown, unappreciative

Answer: B

Explanation: Typically, prefixes and suffixes are usually introduced in second/third grade beginning with the simplest and most commonly occurring morphemes. The prefixes re- and un- in the words rerun, review, unable, and unseen meet these criteria. Option D is incorrect as "unappreciative" is beyond third-grade level.

QUESTION 56

A fourth-grade teacher is going to read a short informational text regarding rocket science. After reading to the whole class, the teacher will pair students to read the same text to each other. Which of the following planned support is NOT used?

A. modeling
B. repetition
C. summarizing
D. paired activity

Answer: C

Explanation: The activity involves the teacher reading, which is modeling. The teacher has the students work in pairs for the reading activity. The students are rereading the informational text, which is repetition. There is no summarizing that is being done in the activity mentioned.

QUESTION 57

A fifth-grade teacher includes instruction in word learning strategies as one component in an interdisciplinary approach to vocabulary development. For example, after the students start reading about plants in a science textbook, the teacher conducts a lesson focused on assisting students learn the concepts and vocabulary introduced in the text. Which of the following word-learning strategies would best develop students' vocabulary?

A. learning a semantic feature analysis
B. using flashcards to learn words
C. reading articles on new words
D. finding facts related to vocabulary words

Answer: A

Explanation: The semantic feature analysis strategy uses a grid to help individuals explore how sets of things are related to one another. Semantic feature analysis supports students in deepening knowledge regarding new words.

QUESTION 58

A sixth-grade teacher writes the words cunning, cumbersome, and astonishing on the Smart Board, and she provides a definition for each of the words. Which of the following steps would be most effective for the teacher to take next to deepen the students' knowledge of the words?

A. having the students repeat the definition
B. showing flashcards and having the students define words
C. having the students write sentences using the words
D. providing examples showing the right and the wrong way of using each word

Answer: D

Explanation: The key in the question is "deepen students' knowledge," which should involve activity that goes beyond defining. By providing examples of appropriate and inappropriate use of the words, the teacher is deepening the students' knowledge.

QUESTION 59

Students in a sixth-grade class read a lengthy newspaper article regarding the importance of uniform policies in schools. After a class discussion of the author's points, the teacher begins a lesson discussing the pros and cons of uniforms in school settings. Which of the following types of graphic organizers would be most effective to use in this lesson?

A. a flowchart
B. an outline
C. a T-chart
D. a Venn-diagram

Answer: C

Explanation: T-Chart is a type of graphic organizer in which a student lists and examines two facets of a topic, like the pros and cons associated with it, its advantages and disadvantages, or facts vs. opinions.

QUESTION 60

Use the poem below by William Shakespeare to answer the question.

"When well-appareled April on the heel
Of limping winter treads."

Which of the following poetic devices is used most prominently in the poem?

A. personification
B. hyperbole
C. simile
D. ambiguity

Answer: A

Explanation: April cannot put on a dress. Winter does not limp. The month of April and the winter season are given two distinct human qualities. Personification is the attribution of a personal nature or human characteristics to something nonhuman.

QUESTION 61

Which of the following sets of words is most closely associated with if/then text structure?

A. since, result, consequently
B. while, yet, similarly
C. in addition, moreover, additionally
D. such as, by, more

Answer: A

Explanation: If/then structure is typically what happens if something happens. This is linked to the words since, result, and consequently.

QUESTION 62

Knowledge of the relationship between letters and sounds is _____.

    A. phonemic awareness
    B. fluency
    C. vocabulary
    D. phonics

Answer: D

Explanation: Knowledge of the relationship between letters and sounds is phonics.

QUESTION 63

A first-grade teacher is spending a portion of the afternoon having students write and draw in personal journals. The students are free to write and draw about any topic they desire. This approach will mainly benefit students by promoting their ability to

    A. think creatively.
    B. think deeply.
    C. get personal.
    D. improve grammar.

Answer: A

Explanation: The students are free to select what they want to draw or write, so the students have the freedom to think more creatively.

QUESTION 64

Which of the following is NOT one of the five essential components of reading identified by the National Reading Panel?

A. phonics
B. fluency
C. vocabulary
D. spelling

Answer: D

Explanation: The five essential components of reading are phonemic awareness, phonics, fluency, vocabulary, and comprehension.

QUESTION 65

Understanding social and emotional aspects is linked mostly to which levels of reading comprehension?

A. lexical comprehension
B. literal comprehension
C. interpretive comprehension
D. affective comprehension

Answer: D

Explanation: Lexical comprehension is understanding key vocabulary in text. Literal comprehension is answering who, what, where, and when questions. Interpretive comprehension is answering what if, why, and how questions. Affection comprehension is understanding social and emotional aspects.

QUESTION 66

Which of the following is NOT an open syllable word?

    A. no
    B. my
    C. fly
    D. hat

Answer: D

Explanation: An open syllable has a vowel at the end of the syllable. A closed syllable is a vowel followed by a consonant. Option D is not an open syllable word.

QUESTION 67

Which of the following is most accurate regarding fiction and nonfiction text?

    A. Fiction can be both narrative and informational.
    B. Nonfiction can be both narrative and informational.
    C. Fiction can be informational only.
    D. Nonfiction can be informational only.

Answer: B

Explanation: Narrative tells a story. Typically, the main character or person in the text faces a problem and tries to resolve the problem. There is a beginning, middle, and end. Informational text is written to describe factual information in an understandable format. Nonfiction can be both narrative and informational while fiction can only be narrative.

QUESTION 68

An elementary teacher has her students read the story "The Mitten." Then, she gives her students a worksheet with images of different animals, and she instructs her students to label the animals below in the order they were introduced in the story. Which of the following reading strategies is being most targeted in this activity?

A. recalling
B. retelling
C. sequencing
D. summarizing

Answer: C

Explanation: Sequencing is a reading strategy that requires students to sequence the events in a story or retell the story in chronological order.

QUESTION 69

An elementary reading teacher is looking to get her students involved in self-assessing their own reading skills. Which of the following is the best activity to accomplish this goal?

A. choral reading
B. taped reading
C. echo reading
D. buddy reading

Answer: B

Explanation: Taped reading is when the teacher tapes the children reading individually. The children can listen back to what they have read. They self-assess their own reading.

QUESTION 70

Which of the following is NOT written in the first person?

    A. autobiography
    B. memoir
    C. personal essay
    D. biography

Answer: D

Explanation: Biography is not written in the first person; it is typically written by someone else.

QUESTION 71

Which of the following is NOT a consonant blend?

    A. bl
    B. br
    C. ar
    D. spl

Answer: C

Explanation: Consonant blends (also called consonant clusters) are groups of two or three consonants in words that make a distinct consonant sound. Option C is not a consonant blend.

QUESTION 72

Since the weather is bad, I'll stay inside for the remainder of the night.

The above sentence is which of the following?

A. simple sentence
B. complex sentence
C. compound sentence
D. compound-complex sentence

Answer: B

Explanation: A complex sentence is a sentence with an independent clause joined by an dependent/subordinate clause.

QUESTION 73

In early elementary grade levels, which of the following methods is important for improving a student's reading fluency?

A. Giving the student easy reading passages to read.
B. Giving the student multiple opportunities to reread the same passages.
C. Teaching the student vocabulary words prior to reading the passages.
D. Providing the student with a summary of the reading passages.

Answer: B

Explanation: Fluency is defined as the ability to read with speed, accuracy, and proper expression. To improve fluency, the best approach is to give the student multiple opportunities to reread the same passage, which allows the student to improve recognition and recall sight words.

QUESTION 74

Some people love cold winters near the fireplace with hot coffee. Others love the hot summer with snow cones and ice cream cones. Write an essay that names your favorite season and give reasons why it is best.

The above prompt is associated with which type of writing?

    A. narrative
    B. descriptive
    C. expository
    D. persuasive

Answer: D

Explanation: Persuasive writing attempts to convince the reader that the point of view recommended by the writer is valid. The prompt best represents persuasive writing.

QUESTION 75

Below is a sample work from a sixth-grade student:

There are many sales going on during the Black Friday Holiday Sales. There are stores that provide many discounts on electronics and clothing. There can be stores that even offer free stuff during the holiday season. There can be so much fun during the holiday period.

Which is NOT an area the student needs improvement in?

    A. word choice
    B. capitalization
    C. sentence structure
    D. spelling

Answer: D

Explanation: The student needs improvement in capitalization due to his capitalization "holiday sales." Each of the sentences start with "there," so the student needs to work on word choices. All sentences used are basic, so sentence structure improvement is needed. No spelling error is shown in the student's work.

QUESTION 76

Jack is having some difficulty in reading as indicated by his score on an oral reading fluency assessment. When he reads, he sometimes inserts words that are not in the text. This shows a weakness in which area of fluency?

A. prosody
B. rate
C. accuracy
D. automaticity

Answer: A

Explanation: Prosody refers to the expressiveness with which a student reads. Jack expresses more words than he needs to, so the student can improve in prosody.

QUESTION 77

More than 70% of a first-grade class scored at high risk on the oral reading fluency assessment. Which instructional practice would be most effective for improving the students' oral reading fluency?

A. daily independent reading in the afternoon
B. peer reading on familiar text
C. vocabulary development on unfamiliar words
D. constantly reading text with corrective feedback

Answer: D

Explanation: Having students read text and providing feedback will support students in oral reading fluency. Option D targets reading in addition to ensuring improvement with constant feedback.

QUESTION 78

While reading a book aloud, one of the students believes the teacher is reading the pictures instead of the words in the book. Which of the following is the student lacking in understanding?

    A. letter movement
    B. phonological awareness
    C. concepts of print
    D. alphabetic principle

Answer: C

Explanation: Since the student thinks the teacher is reading the pictures as opposed to the words, the student lacks understanding of the concept of print. Concepts of print refers to the awareness of how print works.

QUESTION 79

A teacher asks her kindergarten students to say words sound by sound while moving balls for each sound. This approach is showing what instructional method?

    A. intensive instruction
    B. explicit systematic instruction
    C. differentiated instruction
    D. shared reading

Answer: B

Explanation: Explicit instruction is making the skill obvious to the student. Systematic instruction is following a sequence of development for language and reading acquisition.

QUESTION 80

A fifth-grade teacher models how to select unknown words and write explanations, reread areas where they struggle to understand, write questions based on the passages, and infer what will happen in the next passage.

These are examples of comprehension strategies that include:

    A. clarifying, summarizing, questioning, and predicting
    B. clarifying, monitoring, questioning, and predicting
    C. defining, monitoring, previewing, and predicting
    D. clarifying, monitoring, questioning, and previewing

Answer: B

Explanation: The students are asked to write explanations, which is linked to clarifying. The students reread areas they struggle with, which require monitoring weak area development. Writing questions is linked to questioning strategy. Inferring what will happen next is linked to predicting.

This page is intentionally left blank.

PRACTICE EXAM 2

This page is intentionally left blank.

Answer Sheet – Exam 2

Question Numbers	Selected Answer	Question Numbers	Selected Answer	Question Numbers	Selected Answer
1		31		61	
2		32		62	
3		33		63	
4		34		64	
5		35		65	
6		36		66	
7		37		67	
8		38		68	
9		39		69	
10		40		70	
11		41		71	
12		42		72	
13		43		73	
14		44		74	
15		45		75	
16		46		76	
17		47		77	
18		48		78	
19		49		79	
20		50		80	
21		51			
22		52			
23		53			
24		54			
25		55			
26		56			
27		57			
28		58			
29		59			
30		60			

This page is intentionally left blank.

Test 2 - Full Practice Exam Questions

QUESTION 1

A kindergarten teacher is looking to get her students to develop phonological awareness. Which of the following is the most appropriate activity?

- A. writing letters in large font on the smart board
- B. reciting songs with simple rhymes
- C. reciting the alphabet from letter z back to letter a
- D. reading large print materials

Answer:

QUESTION 2

A second-grade teacher is having her students read the folktale titled "The Ant and the Grasshopper." The teacher's goal is to have the students engage in higher-order thinking. After reading half of the folktale, the teacher will ask the students to make a prediction of what they think will happen next. Which level of Bloom's taxonomy does the activity involve?

- A. knowledge
- B. comprehension
- C. application
- D. analysis

Answer:

QUESTION 3

- Can you distinguish between...?
- What differences exist between...?
- Can you provide an example of what you mean...?
- Can you provide a definition for...?

The above questions best demonstrate which level of Bloom's taxonomy?

A. knowledge
B. comprehension
C. synthesis
D. analysis

Answer:

QUESTION 4

Jenny, an elementary teacher, displays anchor charts with key vocabulary words. Prior to reading, Jenny also does a pop quiz regarding the vocabulary words. In addition, she gives each student a copy of the reading materials. Taking these steps best supports her students in which of the following?

A. word knowledge development
B. reading comprehension
C. visual comprehension
D. analyze information

Answer:

QUESTION 5

Below is a conversation between a teacher and her students.

> Teacher: I will point to a letter, and you will tell me its sound.
> [Point to d and gesture.]
> Students: /d/
> Teacher: Correct, /d/.
> [Point to r and gesture.]
> Students: /r/
> Teacher: Yes, /r/.
> [Point to s.]
> Hector, what sound?
> Hector: /s/

Based on the conversation above, which of the following is the teacher targeting in this lesson?

    A. digraphs

    B. vowels

    C. consonants

    D. phonics

Answer:

QUESTION 6

An elementary education teacher is going to teach her students about consonant blends. She starts off by telling her students the following:

You will learn how to read words that have two or three consonants right next to each other. Unlike digraphs, each letter keeps its sound.

If the teacher wanted to explain the importance of this lesson, what can the teacher indicate to the students? Select TWO answers.

    A. helps you read better

    B. helps you spell better

    C. helps you write better

    D. helps you comprehend better

Answer:

QUESTION 7

A first-grade student writes "R ct is rd n bg" and reads aloud "Our cat is red and big." The teacher can improve the student's spelling by implementing which of the following activities?

    A. use anchor charts to show necessary vocabulary words

    B. explain the difference between "our" and "are"

    C. explain that most words have more than 2 letters

    D. give direct instruction on phonics

Answer:

QUESTION 8

A kindergarten teacher is looking to demonstrate the meaning of common prepositional opposites to her students. Which of the following pairs of words is NOT appropriate to use in this demonstration?

    A. south and north

    B. left and right

    C. besides and under

    D. over and under

Answer:

QUESTION 9

A fourth-grade teacher is giving her students the following persuasive writing prompts to select from:

> Writing Prompt 1: Why do you think you should be able to choose your own breakfast?

> Writing Prompt 2: Why do you think fourth graders should spend more time playing outside?

In developing a rubric, which of the following are appropriate to assess? Select THREE answers.

A. grammar
B. organization
C. reasons and supports
D. length

Answer:

QUESTION 10

A second-grade student has drawn a picture of a red bike in her journal and has written: "I HVE RD BKE." Based on the student's work, which of the following is an appropriate next step in the student's development as a writer?

A. use proper punctuation
B. print lowercase letters
C. use medial vowel sounds
D. learn spelling of common words

Answer:

QUESTION 11

Jimmy, a third-grade student, is a visual student. He responds better with visual and interactive materials. He has shown weakness in understanding stories. To support Jimmy in comprehension, which of the following is the most appropriate material to use in reading class?

A. picture book
B. graphic novel
C. chapter book
D. informational text

Answer:

QUESTION 12

Which of the following is the correct word wall to use for homonyms, homophones, and homographs?

A.

	Same sound	Different Sound	Same Spelling	Different Spelling	Same Meaning
Homonyms fair, fair, fair	X		X		
Homophones feet, feat	X			X	
Homographs wind, wind		X	X		

B.

	Same sound	Different Sound	Same Spelling	Different Spelling	Same Meaning
Homonyms fair, fair, fair		X	X		
Homophones feet, feat	X			X	
Homographs wind, wind		X	X		

C.

	Same sound	Different Sound	Same Spelling	Different Spelling	Same Meaning
Homonyms fair, fair, fair	X		X		
Homophones feet, feat	X			X	
Homographs wind, wind		X			X

D.

	Same sound	Different Sound	Same Spelling	Different Spelling	Same Meaning
Homonyms fair, fair, fair	X		X		
Homophones feet, feat		X		X	
Homographs wind, wind		X	X		

Answer:

QUESTION 13

Which of the following activities reflect third-grade students' understanding of making compound words?

    A. Make 15 flashcards of common words that can either stand alone or be combined with another word.
    B. Write an essay that requires the use of compound words.
    C. Have students read a book that includes compound words.
    D. Make a list of ten common words that can stand alone or be broken down into two or more words.

Answer:

QUESTION 14

A fourth-grade teacher is having her students read "Arthur and the Real Mr. Ratburn." After reading, the teacher will have the students fill out the following questions:

• Beginning (characters and setting)
    Who are the main characters in the story?
    Where and when does the story take place?
• Middle (problem)
    What is Arthur's problem?
    How does he try to solve it?
• End (solution and theme)
    How is the problem solved?
    What does Arthur learn about himself?

The above activity best supports the students in

    A. understanding how to solve problems.
    B. developing vocabulary words.
    C. improving comprehension.
    D. making connection to personal experiences.

Answer:

QUESTION 15

Word Cards: saw, was, there, they, for, from, of

A teacher lines up several word cards on a desk. The teacher will say one of the words then have the student point to the word and remove it from the row. The teacher will repeat the activity with another word. Which of the following skills is the activity most likely to develop?

   A. developing vocabulary
   B. recognizing high-frequency words
   C. using context clues
   D. reading words

Answer:

QUESTION 16

The third-grade student has written the following in his notebook:

goed – breaked – fixed

Which of the following best explains the reason for such usage?

   A. The student is using suffixes incorrectly.
   B. The student is reversing a previously acquired rule.
   C. The student is over using a recently learned rule.
   D. The student is not using proper spelling of common words.

Answer:

QUESTION 17

The writing sample below is typical of a particular student's work.

Last week, me and my dad had a fun time at the game. We go to the after party, and we saw a lot of people.

The teacher can best help the student's writing development by reviewing which of the following? Select TWO answers.

    A. tense
    B. spelling
    C. pronouns
    D. syntax

Answer:

QUESTION 18

Which of the following is an example of an internal conflict?

    A. I can't walk in the cold.
    B. Jake and I did not agree on what to eat.
    C. I can't believe I did not speak up in the discussion.
    D. The wind is picking up. Things are going to fly.

Answer:

QUESTION 19

Jake's parents are planning to get Jake two dogs for his birthday next month. Since Jake's family lives in an apartment where animals are not allowed, the family is looking to buy a house. They have decided to get a house with a large backyard for Jake to play with the dogs. Next week, they plan to go to some open houses.

In the passage shown above, which of the following is the predominate pattern of organization?

A. chronological order
B. problem and solution
C. compare and contrast
D. agree and disagree

Answer:

QUESTION 20

While working on a writing assignment, Jake asked Emmy to read his essay and highlight areas that needed more clarifying and expanding along with areas that were too wordy. This activity best reflects which stage of the writing process?

A. proofreading
B. outlining
C. revising
D. publishing

Answer:

QUESTION 21

Which of the following correctly sequences the steps in the writing process?

A. revising, drafting, and proofreading
B. drafting, proofreading, and revising
C. revising, proofreading, and drafting
D. drafting, reviewing, and proofreading

Answer:

QUESTION 22

Which of the following options is part of the drafting process? Select THREE answers.

    A. putting commas in place

    B. crafting full sentences

    C. jotting down notes

    D. using paragraphs

Answer:

QUESTION 23

In writing essays, the "hamburger technique" is used for which of the following?

    A. writing introduction paragraph

    B. writing body paragraph

    C. writing concluding paragraph

    D. writing full essay

Answer:

QUESTION 24

Which of the following students is demonstrating the specific type of phonological awareness known as phonemic awareness?

    A. a student who, being shown the letter "A", can orally identify its corresponding sound

    B. a student who, after hearing the word bat, can orally identify that it ends with the sound /t/

    C. a student who listens to the words bat, cat, fat, and ring and can identify that ring is different

    D. a student who listens to the word encouragement and can determine that it contains multiple syllables

Answer:

QUESTION 25

A teacher is planning to have her students identify if a letter is a consonant or a vowel in different words of different text along with having students apply their knowledge on consonants, vowels, and y's. Which of the following is most likely being exposed to students in this activity?

    A. different types of vowels
    B. vowel diphthongs
    C. types of syllables
    D. vowel-consonant patterns

Answer:

QUESTION 26

Which of the following words show the phonemic awareness skills of recognizing two words that contain the same sound?

    A. bed and jack
    B. thin and path
    C. tag and bed
    D. gate and game

Answer:

QUESTION 27

Below is a passage from the story Pecos Bill (1966).

What Bill planned to do was leap from his horse and grab the cyclone by the neck. But as he came near and saw how high the top of the whirling tower was, he knew he would have to do something better than that. Just as he . . . came close enough to the cyclone to feel its hot breath, a knife of lightning streaked down into the ground. It struck there, quivering, just long enough for Bill to reach out and grab it. As the lightning bolt whipped back up into the sky, Bill held on. When he was as high as the top of the cyclone, he jumped and landed astraddle its black, spinning shoulders.

By then, everyone in Texas, New Mexico, Arizona, and Oklahoma was watching. They saw Bill grab hold of that cyclone's shoulders and haul them back. They saw him wrap his legs around the cyclone's belly and squeeze so hard the cyclone started to pant. Then Bill got out his lasso and slung it around the cyclone's neck. He pulled it tighter and tighter until the cyclone started to choke, spitting out rocks and dust. All the rain that was mixed up in it started to fall.

Which of the following literary devices is strongly supported in the paragraphs above?

    A. metaphor
    B. hyperbole
    C. alliteration
    D. simile

Answer:

QUESTION 28

Use the poem below by William Shakespeare to answer the question.

"Neptune's ocean wash this blood
Clean from my hand? No. This my hand will rather
The multitudinous seas incarnadine,
Making the green one red."

Which of the following poetic devices is used most prominently in the poem?

    A. personification
    B. hyperbole
    C. simile
    D. ambiguity

Answer:

QUESTION 29

                          fear and each
The above pair of words is best described as

    A. open syllable words.
    B. closed syllable words.
    C. vowel paired words.
    D. consonant words.

Answer:

QUESTION 30

Kate loves her cats, and the cats love her too because she feeds them.

The above sentence is which of the following?

A. simple sentence
B. complex sentence
C. compound sentence
D. compound-complex sentence

Answer:

QUESTION 31

"A crow was sitting on a branch of a tree with a piece of cheese in her beak when a fox observed her and set his wits to work to discover some way of getting the cheese. Coming and standing under the tree he looked up and said, 'What a noble bird I see above me! Her beauty is without equal…' Down came the cheese, of course, and the Fox, snatching it up, said, 'You have a voice, madam, I see: what you want is wits.'"

The above is an example of which of the following?

A. fable
B. tall tales
C. myths
D. ethos

Answer:

QUESTION 32

_____ is automatic word recognizing, rapid decoding, and checking for meaning.

A. Decode
B. Fluency
C. Fallacious reasoning
D. Comprehension

Answer:

106

QUESTION 33

The following is from a third-grade student writing:

In the middle of the night, James quickly woke up when he heard a noise, and he ran to his son's room.

Select the parts of speech used in the sentence above.

    A. noun
    B. pronoun
    C. verb
    D. adverb
    E. preposition
    F. conjunction

Answer:

QUESTION 34

Which of the following correctly orders the writing development phases?

    A. picture writing – scribble writing – random letter – invented spelling – conventional writing
    B. scribble writing – picture writing – random letter – invented spelling – conventional writing
    C. random writing – scribble writing – picture letter – invented spelling – conventional writing
    D. scribble writing – random writing – picture letter – invented spelling – conventional writing

Answer:

QUESTION 35

An elementary education teacher is planning to have students listen to stories and retell stories. It is most likely that the teacher is attempting to engage the student in

A. understanding syntax.
B. comprehension of text.
C. phonological knowledge.
D. read information text.

Answer:

QUESTION 36

Activity: timed repeated readings of independent level text, paired readings, readers' theatre, expert reading, and poetry reading

The above activity is most closely related to which instructional goal?

A. fluency – speed and accuracy
B. word study – sort words by vowel sounds
C. comprehension – strategies for reading comprehension
D. writing – express ideas in writing

Answer:

QUESTION 37

Teacher: It is very dark in here. There are squeaky sounds. I also feel something sticky touching me. I am really scared. Where am I?

Student: haunted house

Teacher: I hear screaming and my stomach feels really funny. Do you see my hair blowing. I am super excited. Where am I?

Student: amusement park

Which of the following is the teacher attempting to evaluate?

- A. inferring
- B. comprehending
- C. predicting
- D. organizing

Answer:

QUESTION 38

How many morpheme(s) are in the word bananas?

- A. one
- B. two
- C. three
- D. four

Answer:

QUESTION 39

Which of the following students composed both sentences as simple sentences?

- A. Jenny: I am tall. Super smart.
- B. Clair: I live there. I am here.
- C. Alexis: Run fast! We will be late.
- D. Kiki: Jump up. He will win.

Answer:

QUESTION 40

A dependent clause is needed in which of the following? Select TWO answers.

- A. simple sentence
- B. compound sentence
- C. complex sentence
- D. compound-complex sentence

Answer:

QUESTION 41

cake – fake – make – bake – snake

The above words share all the following except?

- A. rime
- B. vowel
- C. morpheme
- D. long-vowel /e/ digraph

Answer:

QUESTION 42

Which of the following versions of a sentence from a student's draft of an expository essay would be most effective for the student to use to convey an idea clearly and concisely?

   A. Blue birds are tiny and delicate. During migration, they can fly as far as 1000 miles one way.

   B. Blue birds are tiny, seemingly delicate creatures, but during migration they can fly as far as 1000 miles one way.

   C. Due to their tiny size, few would know that blue birds have the ability to fly as far as 1000 miles one way.

   D. Blue birds may be tiny but they have features that include migrating as far as 1000 miles one way.

Answer:

QUESTION 43

Objective: The students are to write paragraph(s) that introduce an opinion, with concluding statements that explain why a certain action needs to be taken.

Which of the following activities would be most appropriate for the second-grade students to work on for the objective?

   A. read an opinion statement and summarize it

   B. write a letter to the principal in response to the new uniform policy

   C. write an essay on the impact of the American Revolution

   D. research a topic related to the best cooking show

Answer:

QUESTION 44

A sixth-grade teacher is looking to monitor students' progress related to explaining the relationship between few concepts in an informational text by drawing on precise information in the text. Which of the following assessments would be most beneficial for the teacher to use for this purpose?

A. open-ended questions that test students' ability on inferential comprehension related to information text

B. in-class discussions of key concepts followed by independent writing assignment involving citing details from text when making connection between concepts

C. in-class discussions of key concepts followed by group writing assignment involving citing details from text when making connection between concepts

D. open-ended questions that test students' ability on literal comprehension related to information text

Answer:

QUESTION 45

Which factor contributes the most in reading comprehension acquisition among students in the first-grade?

A. concept of print

B. vocabulary development

C. decoding skills

D. oral language development

Answer:

QUESTION 46

Use the excerpt below from a small-group discussion to answer the question that follows.

Student 1: Okay, let's work together to get this poster completed. We can all do something for the post. I think I will draw.
Student 2: Do you mean draw the content or pictures, or both?
Student 1: Just the pictures. Do you want to write the content?
Student 3: I can help with the content. What are you going to draw?
Student 2: I will help with the content too.
Student 1: I will draw the cat and dog.

The excerpt best exemplifies which of the following forms of interpersonal communications?

A. analyzing
B. clarifying
C. confirming
D. completing

Answer:

QUESTION 47

Martha really needed to get to the bus, so she ran like the wind.

The sentence above uses which of the following literary element?

A. simile
B. personification
C. oxymoron
D. hyperbole

Answer:

QUESTION 48

An elementary reading teacher is going to have her students read an informational text about the tropical rainforest. Prior to reading the informational text, the teacher is going to review academic vocabulary words. Why is it important to teach academic vocabulary to students at the elementary grade levels?

    A. Such vocabulary is very difficult to articulate.

    B. Such vocabulary relates to students who are visual.

    C. Such vocabulary is not typically used during informal conversation.

    D. Such vocabulary is completely unknown to students and using context clues to determine meaning is impossible.

Answer:

QUESTION 49

Kelly is willing to run in the hot sun, but Jack is <u>reluctant</u> and goes inside because of the hot temperatures.

Which type of context clue in the sentence helps decode the meaning of the underlined word?

    A. contrast

    B. furthermore

    C. example

    D. definition

Answer:

QUESTION 50

A teacher is informally assessing third-grade students' listening comprehension skills after reading aloud the fable "The Rat and the Elephant." Which of the following prompts requires the students to draw an inference from the fable?

A. Who are the characters in the fable?
B. What is the rat used to?
C. How does the cat demonstrate how the rat is not as impressive as the elephant?
D. What lesson does the fable teach?

Answer:

QUESTION 51

Month	Week 1	Week 2	Week 3
Child's spelling of "coat"	ct	cot	cote

Based on the information in the chart above, it can be inferred that the child is

A. unaware of the relationship between letters and sounds.
B. unaware of the concept of alphabetic principle.
C. progressing related to the relationship between letters and sounds.
D. progressing on the concept of alphabetic principle.

Answer:

QUESTION 52

After reading a picture book regarding the different weather seasons with a class of kindergartners, a teacher talks about the seasons. Then, the teacher instructs the students to use the pictures in the book to talk about seasons with their peers. The teacher's approach best allows oral language development in young students by

    A. helping them understand their environment.
    B. promoting them to engage in conversation.
    C. using texts to relate to their personal lives.
    D. helping them think-aloud to encourage thought.

Answer:

QUESTION 53

Students have written their first draft for the writing prompt provided by their teacher. Which of the following strategies would be the next most beneficial for the students?

    A. rereading independently the essay
    B. checking if ideas are correctly written
    C. holding peer conferences
    D. adding more details to paragraphs

Answer:

QUESTION 54

Jimmy is a fifth-grade student, and his English teacher is going to have him present his research on bowling to his classmates. Jimmy is very shy and nervous about presenting in front of his classmates. To support Jimmy, which of the following is the most helpful?

    A. memorize everything for the presentation
    B. type everything that he will say in the presentation
    C. write keywords on note cards to use during presentation
    D. write vocabulary words he has difficulty understanding

Answer:

QUESTION 55

An elementary education teacher is having her students read Belling the Cat. After reading, the teacher has her students write a summary of the story. What is the primary purpose of this activity?

    A. to see if the students understand key vocabulary words
    B. to see if students comprehend the text
    C. to see if the students can write properly
    D. to see if the students have good fluency rate

Answer:

QUESTION 56

Which of the following concepts involves understanding the letter-sound or sound-symbol relationships of language and helps readers to sound out unknown words?

    A. graphophonic cues
    B. morphology
    C. phonemic awareness
    D. syntax

Answer:

QUESTION 57

Which of the following is NOT an imperative sentence?

    A. Please pass the water.
    B. Don't write too much.
    C. I need to eat bread.
    D. Go to mom's house.

Answer:

QUESTION 58

Which of the following accurately describes footnotes or endnotes? Selection TWO answers.

    A. Footnotes appear at the bottom of each page they refer to.

    B. Footnotes appear at the very end of a text.

    C. Endnotes appear at the bottom of each page they refer to.

    D. Endnotes appear at the very end of a text.

Answer:

QUESTION 59

Billy's dad, a farmer, owns land in Texas. Which of the following resources is best for Billy's dad?

    A. dictionary

    B. atlas

    C. almanac

    D. thesaurus

Answer:

QUESTION 60

The following is a selection from Alfred Noyes' poem "The Highwayman."

The wind was a torrent of darkness among the gusty trees.
The moon was a ghostly galleon tossed upon cloudy seas.
The road was a ribbon of moonlight over the purple moor,
And the highwayman came riding—
Riding—riding—
The highwayman came riding, up to the old inn-door.

He'd a French cocked-hat on his forehead, a bunch of lace at his chin,
A coat of the claret velvet, and breeches of brown doe-skin.
They fitted with never a wrinkle. His boots were up to the thigh.
And he rode with a jewelled twinkle,
His pistol butts a-twinkle,
His rapier hilt a-twinkle, under the jewelled sky.

What is the rhyme scheme for the above poem?

   A. aabccb

   B. ababab

   C. aaccbb

   D. aacbcb

Answer:

QUESTION 61

Which of the following require the need to cite reference material? Select TWO answers.

   A. using quotations

   B. paraphrasing

   C. documenting conversations

   D. stating facts

Answer:

QUESTION 62

Which of the following writing development phases is shown in the sample above?

   A. picture writing

   B. scribble writing

   C. random letter

   D. invented spelling

Answer:

QUESTION 63

For a project regarding painting techniques of Vincent van Gogh for upper elementary students, which of the following is the most appropriate keyword to search when looking for resources on the internet or library catalog?

   A. art

   B. painting

   C. techniques

   D. Vincent van Gogh

Answer:

QUESTION 64

Which of the following is the most effective way to develop decoding, fluency, vocabulary development, text comprehension, and learner engagement?

   A. choral reading

   B. round-robin reading

   C. readers theatre

   D. repeated reading

Answer:

QUESTION 65

A fourth-grade teacher asks the students to partner to read a literary selection. The teacher puts a few questions on a worksheet for students to answer while reading the story. Which type of assessment is the teacher using?

A. informal
B. formal
C. diagnostic
D. standardized

Answer:

QUESTION 66

Which of the following modes of writing is intended to provide a story about a friend's birthday party experience?

A. descriptive
B. narrative
C. expository
D. persuasive

Answer:

QUESTION 67

A first-grade teacher starts a reading activity by pointing out the title, author, illustrator, and title page. Which skill is this teacher most likely targeting?

A. generating ideas
B. expanding vocabulary
C. concepts about words
D. concepts about books

Answer:

QUESTION 68

Which of the following is the best demonstration of phonemic segmenting from first-grade students working with the word "bumping"?

    A. bump-ing

    B. bu-mp-ing

    C. bum-pi-ng

    D. b-u-m-p-i-n-g

Answer:

QUESTION 69

An elementary education student is interested in the following from a book:

- overview of text
- relationship among topics
- organization of the text

The best place for the student to look at in the text is which of the following?

    A. footnotes

    B. glossary

    C. index

    D. table of contents

Answer:

QUESTION 70

In order to prepare students to read about different animals, the teacher organized a field trip to the local zoo and arranged a presentation by the zoo master for the class. The teacher is developing

    A. background information and purpose.
    B. interest and motivation.
    C. oral language skills.
    D. background information, presentation skills, and purpose.

Answer:

QUESTION 71

A third-grade teacher has been using a number of anecdotal records compiled over several months about a student. From the information, the teacher notes that the student is having trouble with pronouns and nouns agreement and develops a set of remediation activities for that student. Which of the following responses is an example of another qualitative measure to use for assessment purposes?

    A. summative assessments
    B. diagnostic assessments
    C. equitable assessments
    D. portfolio assessments

Answer:

QUESTION 72

- coming ready for discussion
- staying on topic
- maintaining eye-contact

The above best supports students in

A. ensuring the audience's comprehension.
B. getting to learn more about audience.
C. helping sell the topic.
D. speaking better

Answer:

QUESTION 73

_____ are objects and materials from everyday life, especially when used as teaching aids.

A. Modeling
B. Dictation
C. Realia
D. Role playing

Answer:

QUESTION 74

Teacher: What is the first sound in ban?

Student: The first sound is /b/.

The above represents which of the following phonemic-awareness strategies?

A. isolation
B. categorization
C. blending
D. segmentation

Answer:

QUESTION 75

do – said – was – of

The above list best represent which of the following?

A. regular words
B. passive words
C. irregular words
D. active words

Answer:

QUESTION 76

In a kindergarten class, the teacher reads "Playing with Friends" aloud, while the students echo the words the teacher has read. Which of the following approaches to reading is being undertaken in this activity?

A. guided reading
B. shared reading
C. active reading
D. round robin

Answer:

QUESTION 77

The following is an excerpt from second-grade student's work.

Betty and her friend are going to play, so there are not board. There are excited about the fun day. There have a good planned out day.

The above sentence shows that the student needs help in which of the following?

A. homophones
B. phonics
C. antonyms
D. synonyms

Answer:

QUESTION 78

Which of the following spelling patterns is found in the word "poke"?

    A. CV

    B. CVC

    C. CVCe

    D. CVVC

Answer:

QUESTION 79

The following is a writing piece from a student's journal:

    We had a good vacation. We went in the car for the trip. We saw many nice buildings.

To help the student improve the writing piece, what instructional strategy is the best?

    A. explain the concept of using various types of sentences

    B. ask questions about the vacation

    C. show student examples of good and concise sentences

    D. ask questions about the car

Answer:

QUESTION 80

Which of the following diagrams can not be used to assist students in identifying main ideas?

A.

B.

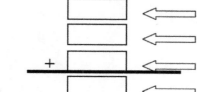

C.

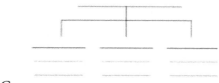

D.

Answer:

This page is intentionally left blank.

Answer Key – Exam 2

Question Numbers	Correct Answer	Question Numbers	Correct Answer	Question Numbers	Correct Answer
1	B	31	A	61	A and B
2	D	32	B	62	B
3	B	33	ABCDEF	63	D
4	B	34	A	64	B
5	C	35	B	65	B
6	A and B	36	A	66	B
7	D	37	A	67	D
8	A	38	B	68	D
9	A,B, and C	39	B	69	D
10	C	40	C and D	70	A
11	B	41	D	71	D
12	A	42	B	72	A
13	A	43	B	73	C
14	C	44	B	74	A
15	B	45	C	75	C
16	C	46	B	76	B
17	A and C	47	A	77	A
18	C	48	C	78	C
19	B	49	A	79	B
20	C	50	D	80	D
21	B	51	C		
22	A, B, and D	52	B		
23	B	53	C		
24	B	54	C		
25	D	55	B		
26	B	56	A		
27	B	57	C		
28	B	58	A and D		
29	C	59	C		
30	D	60	A		

NOTE: Getting approximately 80% of the questions correct increases chances of obtaining passing score on the real exam. This varies from different states and university programs.

This page is intentionally left blank.

Test 2 - Full Practice Exam Questions and Explanations

QUESTION 1

A kindergarten teacher is looking to get her students to develop phonological awareness. Which of the following is the most appropriate activity?

- A. writing letters in large font on the smart board
- B. reciting songs with simple rhymes
- C. reciting the alphabet from letter z back to letter a
- D. reading large print materials

Answer: B

Explanation: Mastery in phonemes is critical to speak and to read. At the kindergarten level, hearing sounds over and over and repeating them supports in establishing basic foundational skills. When reciting songs with simple rhymes, the students are making the sounds of the language that a teacher is encouraging them to imitate. Option B is the most appropriate as the keyword in the question is "develop." The other options do not target developing phonological awareness.

QUESTION 2

A second-grade teacher is having her students read the folktale titled "The Ant and the Grasshopper." The teacher's goal is to have the students engage in higher-order thinking. After reading half of the folktale, the teacher will ask the students to make a prediction of what they think will happen next. Which level of Bloom's taxonomy does the activity involve?

- A. knowledge
- B. comprehension
- C. application
- D. analysis

Answer: D

Explanation: Analysis is to breakdown objects or ideas into simpler parts and find evidence to support generalizations. Because the teacher is asking the students to predict, the students will have to analyze information from the story to make that prediction.

QUESTION 3

- Can you distinguish between...?
- What differences exist between...?
- Can you provide an example of what you mean...?
- Can you provide a definition for...?

The above questions best demonstrate which level of Bloom's taxonomy?

A. knowledge
B. comprehension
C. synthesis
D. analysis

Answer: B

Explanation: Comprehension is the demonstration and understanding of the facts, and all the questions involve demonstrating or showing comprehension.

QUESTION 4

Jenny, an elementary teacher, displays anchor charts with key vocabulary words. Prior to reading, Jenny also does a pop quiz regarding the vocabulary words. In addition, she gives each student a copy of the reading materials. Taking these steps best supports her students in which of the following?

A. word knowledge development
B. reading comprehension
C. visual comprehension
D. analyze information

Answer: B

Explanation: Displaying anchor charts and assessing students on vocabulary words shows that the teacher is invested in ensuring the students understand the reading material. The teacher's approach supports the students in reading comprehension.

QUESTION 5

Below is a conversation between a teacher and her students.

> Teacher: I will point to a letter, and you will tell me its sound.
> [Point to d and gesture.]
> Students: /d/
> Teacher: Correct, /d/.
> [Point to r and gesture.]
> Students: /r/
> Teacher: Yes, /r/.
> [Point to s.]
> Hector, what sound?
> Hector: /s/

Based on the conversation above, which of the following is the teacher targeting in this lesson?

A. digraphs

B. vowels

C. consonants

D. phonics

Answer: C

Explanation: Based on the conversation, the teacher is focusing on consonants. Letters "d", "r", and "s" are consonants. Nothing suggest that the teacher is supporting digraphs, vowels, or phonics.

QUESTION 6

An elementary education teacher is going to teach her students about consonant blends. She starts off by telling her students the following:

You will learn how to read words that have two or three consonants right next to each other. Unlike digraphs, each letter keeps its sound.

If the teacher wanted to explain the importance of this lesson, what can the teacher indicate to the students? Select TWO answers.

    A. helps you read better
    B. helps you spell better
    C. helps you write better
    D. helps you comprehend better

Answer: A and B

Explanation: The lesson of consonant blends is important as longer and more difficult words contain consonant blends, so with this skill, students are able to read and spell more words.

QUESTION 7

A first-grade student writes "R ct is rd n bg" and reads aloud "Our cat is red and big." The teacher can improve the student's spelling by implementing which of the following activities?

    A. use anchor charts to show necessary vocabulary words
    B. explain the difference between "our" and "are"
    C. explain that most words have more than 2 letters
    D. give direct instruction on phonics

Answer: D

Explanation: Teaching the relationship between letters and phonemes to retrieve the pronunciation of words or to spell words is critical to improve spelling.

QUESTION 8

A kindergarten teacher is looking to demonstrate the meaning of common prepositional opposites to her students. Which of the following pairs of words is NOT appropriate to use in this demonstration?

A. south and north
B. left and right
C. besides and under
D. over and under

Answer: A

Explanation: The question refers to kindergarten students. All the options relate to common prepositional opposites, but Option A is not grade appropriate.

QUESTION 9

A fourth-grade teacher is giving her students the following persuasive writing prompts to select from:

Writing Prompt 1: Why do you think you should be able to choose your own breakfast?

Writing Prompt 2: Why do you think fourth graders should spend more time playing outside?

In developing a rubric, which of the following are appropriate to assess? Select THREE answers.

A. grammar
B. organization
C. reasons and supports
D. length

Answer: A, B, and C

Explanation: In all writing, grammar is critical. When writing essays, organization is important, such as introduction, body paragraphs, and conclusion. Supports and reasons are important to include in persuasive writing. Length is not necessarily an indication of writing skills.

QUESTION 10

A second-grade student has drawn a picture of a red bike in her journal and has written: "I HVE RD BKE." Based on the student's work, which of the following is an appropriate next step in the student's development as a writer?

    A. use proper punctuation

    B. print lowercase letters

    C. use medial vowel sounds

    D. learn spelling of common words

Answer: C

Explanation: The student's work shows that the student is not using vowels between consonants. The student knows the alphabet, and the student now needs to include more of the sounds that are actually in the words written.

QUESTION 11

Jimmy, a third-grade student, is a visual student. He responds better with visual and interactive materials. He has shown weakness in understanding stories. To support Jimmy in comprehension, which of the following is the most appropriate material to use in reading class?

    A. picture book

    B. graphic novel

    C. chapter book

    D. informational text

Answer: B

Explanation: A graphic novel is a narrative work in which the story is conveyed to the reader using sequential art. Since Jimmy is a visual student and has difficulty comprehending stories, the best material to use is a graphic novel. In addition, a graphic novel is a grade appropriate resource to use as opposed to a picture book.

QUESTION 12

Which of the following is the correct word wall to use for homonyms, homophones, and homographs?

A.

	Same sound	Different Sound	Same Spelling	Different Spelling	Same Meaning
Homonyms fair, fair, fair	X		X		
Homophones feet, feat	X			X	
Homographs wind, wind		X	X		

B.

	Same sound	Different Sound	Same Spelling	Different Spelling	Same Meaning
Homonyms fair, fair, fair		X	X		
Homophones feet, feat	X			X	
Homographs wind, wind		X	X		

C.

	Same sound	Different Sound	Same Spelling	Different Spelling	Same Meaning
Homonyms fair, fair, fair	X		X		
Homophones feet, feat	X			X	
Homographs wind, wind		X			X

D.

	Same sound	Different Sound	Same Spelling	Different Spelling	Same Meaning
Homonyms fair, fair, fair	X		X		
Homophones feet, feat		X		X	
Homographs wind, wind		X	X		

Answer: A

Explanation: A homograph is a word that has the same spelling as another word but has a different sound and a different meaning. A homophone is a word that has the same sound as another word but is spelled differently and has a different meaning. Homonyms are two words that are spelled the same and sound the same but have different meanings. The table in Option A is accurately reflecting homograph, homophone, and homonym.

QUESTION 13

Which of the following activities reflect third-grade students' understanding of making compound words?

A. Make 15 flashcards of common words that can either stand alone or be combined with another word.
B. Write an essay that requires the use of compound words.
C. Have students read a book that includes compound words.
D. Make a list of ten common words that can stand alone or be broken down into two or more words.

Answer: A

Explanation: Compound words are words that can stand alone or can be combined. The activity in Option A best indicates assessing students knowledge related to compound words.

QUESTION 14

A fourth-grade teacher is having her students read "Arthur and the Real Mr. Ratburn." After reading, the teacher will have the students fill out the following questions:

- Beginning (characters and setting)
    Who are the main characters in the story?
    Where and when does the story take place?
- Middle (problem)
    What is Arthur's problem?
    How does he try to solve it?
- End (solution and theme)
    How is the problem solved?
    What does Arthur learn about himself?

The above activity best supports the students in

    A. understanding how to solve problems.
    B. developing vocabulary words.
    C. improving comprehension.
    D. making connections to personal experiences.

Answer: C

Explanation: The questions indicate that the teacher is going to have students complete a story mapping activity. Story mapping activity supports students in comprehension as the students are looking at the beginning, middle, and end.

QUESTION 15

Word Cards: saw, was, there, they, for, from, of

A teacher lines up several word cards on a desk. The teacher will say one of the words then have the student point to the word and remove it from the row. The teacher will repeat the activity with another word. Which of the following skills is the activity most likely to develop?

A. developing vocabulary
B. recognizing high-frequency words
C. using context clues
D. reading words

Answer: B

Explanation: The words that are used in the activity are high-frequency words, which means that the words are commonly used.

QUESTION 16

The third-grade student has written the following in his notebook:

goed – breaked – fixed

Which of the following best explains the reason for such usage?

A. The student is using suffixes incorrectly.
B. The student is reversing a previously acquired rule.
C. The student is over using a recently learned rule.
D. The student is not using proper spelling of common words.

Answer: C

Explanation: The student is adding "ed" to the end of the words, which is not correctly used in "goed" and "breaked." The student has not acquired knowledge of the exceptions to the rule of using "ed." For example, "breaked" needs to be "broken," and "goed" needs to be "went."

QUESTION 17

The writing sample below is typical of a particular student's work.

Last week, me and my dad had a fun time at the game. We go to the after party, and we saw a lot of people.

The teacher can best help the student's writing development by reviewing which of the following? Select TWO answers.

A. tense
B. spelling
C. pronouns
D. syntax

Answer: A and C

Explanation: The word "go" needs to be "went" as the events happened in the past. In addition, the proper order and use of pronouns is "my dad and I" instead of "me and my dad."

QUESTION 18

Which of the following is an example of an internal conflict?

A. I can't walk in the cold.
B. Jake and I did not agree on what to eat.
C. I can't believe I did not speak up in the discussion.
D. The wind is picking up. Things are going to fly.

Answer: C

Explanation: Internal conflict, which takes place in a person's mind—for example, a struggle to make a decision or overcome a feeling. External conflict generally takes place between a person and someone or something else.

QUESTION 19

Jake's parents are planning to get Jake two dogs for his birthday next month. Since Jake's family lives in an apartment where animals are not allowed, the family is looking to buy a house. They have decided to get a house with a large backyard for Jake to play with the dogs. Next week, they plan to go to some open houses.

In the passage shown above, which of the following is the predominant pattern of organization?

    A. chronological order

    B. problem and solution

    C. compare and contrast

    D. agree and disagree

Answer: B

Explanation: Jake's parents are going to get him dogs for his birthday, but the apartment policy is no animals. To solve this problem, they will look for a house with a large yard for the dogs.

QUESTION 20

While working on a writing assignment, Jake asked Emmy to read his essay and highlight areas that needed more clarifying and expanding along with areas that were too wordy. This activity best reflects which stage of the writing process?

    A. proofreading

    B. outlining

    C. revising

    D. publishing

Answer: C

Explanation: The draft is written, and Jake is having Emmy read it to provide suggestions for improvement. This is the revising stage in the writing process.

QUESTION 21

Which of the following correctly sequences the steps in the writing process?

- A. revising, drafting, and proofreading
- B. drafting, proofreading, and revising
- C. revising, proofreading, and drafting
- D. drafting, reviewing, and proofreading

Answer: B

Explanation: Revising comes after drafting and proofreading, so the answer is Option B.

QUESTION 22

Which of the following options is part of the drafting process? Select THREE answers.

- A. putting commas in place
- B. crafting full sentences
- C. jotting down notes
- D. using paragraphs

Answer: A, B, and D

Explanation: Jotting down notes is done during the brainstorming and pre-writing stages. The drafting process involves putting commas, crafting sentences, and using paragraphs.

QUESTION 23

In writing essays, the "hamburger technique" is used for which of the following?

    A. writing introduction paragraph
    B. writing body paragraph
    C. writing concluding paragraph
    D. writing full essay

Answer: B

Explanation: The hamburger technique is used for writing body paragraphs. The top bun is the topic sentence, which clearly states the paragraph's main idea. The condiments are the evidence, which includes quotes & paraphrased information from sources. Cheese, pickles, onions, lettuce, tomato, and burger is the analysis, which is the bulk of the paragraph. Bottom bun is the sentence relating the paragraph back to the topic sentence and transitioning to the next body paragraph.

QUESTION 24

Which of the following students is demonstrating the specific type of phonological awareness known as phonemic awareness?

    A. a student who, being shown the letter "A", can orally identify its corresponding sound
    B. a student who, after hearing the word bat, can orally identify that it ends with the sound /t/
    C. a student who listens to the words bat, cat, fat, and ring and can identify that ring is different
    D. a student who listens to the word encouragement and can determine that it contains multiple syllables

Answer: B

Explanation: Phonemic awareness is the recognition that spoken words are made up of phonemes—the discrete speech sounds of a language. Being able to identify the ending of a sound shows phonemic awareness.

QUESTION 25

A teacher is planning to have her students identify if a letter is a consonant or a vowel in different words of different text along with having students apply their knowledge on consonants, vowels, and y's. Which of the following is most likely being exposed to students in this activity?

A. different types of vowels
B. vowel diphthongs
C. types of syllables
D. vowel-consonant patterns

Answer: D

Explanation: The activity is getting students exposed to vowel-consonant patterns as the students identify consonant or vowel in different words.

QUESTION 26

Which of the following words show the phonemic awareness skills of recognizing two words that contain the same sound?

A. bed and jack
B. thin and path
C. tag and bed
D. gate and game

Answer: B

Explanation: The words thin and path are two words that contain the same sound.

QUESTION 27

Below is a passage from the story Pecos Bill (1966).

What Bill planned to do was leap from his horse and grab the cyclone by the neck. But as he came near and saw how high the top of the whirling tower was, he knew he would have to do something better than that. Just as he . . . came close enough to the cyclone to feel its hot breath, a knife of lightning streaked down into the ground. It struck there, quivering, just long enough for Bill to reach out and grab it. As the lightning bolt whipped back up into the sky, Bill held on. When he was as high as the top of the cyclone, he jumped and landed astraddle its black, spinning shoulders.

By then, everyone in Texas, New Mexico, Arizona, and Oklahoma was watching. They saw Bill grab hold of that cyclone's shoulders and haul them back. They saw him wrap his legs around the cyclone's belly and squeeze so hard the cyclone started to pant. Then Bill got out his lasso and slung it around the cyclone's neck. He pulled it tighter and tighter until the cyclone started to choke, spitting out rocks and dust. All the rain that was mixed up in it started to fall.

Which of the following literary devices is strongly supported in the paragraphs above?

   A. metaphor
   B. hyperbole
   C. alliteration
   D. simile

Answer: B

Explanation: Hyperbole is a figure of speech in which exaggerated statements or claims are not meant to be taken literally. Hyperbole is shown with statements like "They saw him wrap his legs around the cyclone's belly and squeeze so hard the cyclone started to pant."

QUESTION 28

Use the poem below by William Shakespeare to answer the question.

"Neptune's ocean wash this blood
Clean from my hand? No. This my hand will rather
The multitudinous seas incarnadine,
Making the green one red."

Which of the following poetic devices is used most prominently in the poem?

  A. personification
  B. hyperbole
  C. simile
  D. ambiguity

Answer: B

Explanation: Hyperbole is a figure of speech that involves an exaggeration of ideas for the sake of emphasis. Macbeth, the tragic hero, feels the intolerable prick of his conscience after murdering the king. He feels bad about his sin, and thinks that even the oceans of the greatest magnitude cannot wash the blood of the king off his hands.

QUESTION 29

fear and each

The above pair of words is best described as

  A. open syllable words.
  B. closed syllable words.
  C. vowel paired words.
  D. consonant words.

Answer: C

Explanation: A vowel pair is two vowel letters together that make just one sound.

QUESTION 30

Kate loves her cats, and the cats love her too because she feeds them.

The above sentence is which of the following?

    A. simple sentence
    B. complex sentence
    C. compound sentence
    D. compound-complex sentence

Answer: D

Explanation: Compound-complex sentences contain at least two independent clauses (like a compound sentence) and at least one dependent clause (like a complex sentence).

QUESTION 31

"A crow was sitting on a branch of a tree with a piece of cheese in her beak when a fox observed her and set his wits to work to discover some way of getting the cheese. Coming and standing under the tree he looked up and said, 'What a noble bird I see above me! Her beauty is without equal…' Down came the cheese, of course, and the Fox, snatching it up, said, 'You have a voice, madam, I see: what you want is wits.'"

The above is an example of which of the following?

    A. fable
    B. tall tales
    C. myths
    D. ethos

Answer: A

Explanation: Fable is a literary device that can be defined as a concise and brief story intended to provide a moral lesson at the end. In this excerpt, Aesop provides a moral lesson that flatterers must not be trusted.

QUESTION 32

_____ is automatic word recognizing, rapid decoding, and checking for meaning.

- A. Decode
- B. Fluency
- C. Fallacious reasoning
- D. Comprehension

Answer: B

Explanation: Fluency is automatic word recognizing, rapid decoding, and checking for meaning.

QUESTION 33

The following is from a third-grade student's writing:

In the middle of the night, James quickly woke up when he heard a noise, and he ran to his son's room.

Select the parts of speech used in the sentence above.

- A. noun
- B. pronoun
- C. verb
- D. adverb
- E. preposition
- F. conjunction

Answer: A, B, C, D, E, F

Explanation: All options are used in the sentence. The noun is James. Pronoun is he. Verb is woke. The adverb is quickly. Preposition is to. Conjunction is and.

QUESTION 34

Which of the following correctly orders the writing development phases?

    A. picture writing – scribble writing – random letter – invented spelling – conventional writing

    B. scribble writing – picture writing – random letter – invented spelling – conventional writing

    C. random writing – scribble writing – picture letter – invented spelling – conventional writing

    D. scribble writing – random writing – picture letter – invented spelling – conventional writing

Answer: A

Explanation: Picture writing is the first phase in the writing development followed by scribble writing and then random letter. After that, students invent spelling and finally go into the conventional writing phase.

QUESTION 35

An elementary education teacher is planning to have students listen to stories and retell stories. It is most likely that the teacher is attempting to engage the student in

    A. understanding syntax.
    B. comprehension of text.
    C. phonological knowledge.
    D. read information text.

Answer: B

Explanation: Having the students retell a story is an informal way to assess reading comprehension.

QUESTION 36

Activity: timed repeated readings of independent level text, paired readings, readers' theatre, expert reading, and poetry reading

The above activity is most closely related to which instructional goal?

A. fluency – speed and accuracy
B. word study – sort words by vowel sounds
C. comprehension – strategies for reading comprehension
D. writing – express ideas in writing

Answer: A

Explanation: Fluency is defined as the ability to read with speed, accuracy, and proper expression. This activity is timed and repeated, which is a clear indication that the instructional goal is fluency.

QUESTION 37

Teacher: It is very dark in here. There are squeaky sounds. I also feel something sticky touching me. I am really scared. Where am I?

Student: haunted house

Teacher: I hear screaming and my stomach feels really funny. Do you see my hair blowing. I am super excited. Where am I?

Student: amusement park

Which of the following is the teacher attempting to evaluate?

A. inferring
B. comprehending
C. predicting
D. organizing

Answer: A

Explanation: The teacher is giving clues in the statement of her location, and asks the student to use the clue to determine the location. This involves inferring skills.

QUESTION 38

How many morpheme(s) are in the word bananas?

    A. one

    B. two

    C. three

    D. four

Answer: B

Explanation: Morpheme is a meaningful morphological unit of a language that cannot be further divided. "Bananas" has two morphemes (banana and s).

QUESTION 39

Which of the following students composed both sentences as simple sentences?

    A. Jenny: I am tall. Super smart.

    B. Clair: I live there. I am here.

    C. Alexis: Run fast! We will be late.

    D. Kiki: Jump up. He will win.

Answer: B

Explanation: Simple sentence contains a subject and a verb. Option B has two sentences that include a subject and a verb. In the first sentence, "I" is the subject, and "live" is the verb. In the second sentence, "I" is the subject, and "am" is the verb.

QUESTION 40

A dependent clause is needed in which of the following? Select TWO answers.

A. simple sentence
B. compound sentence
C. complex sentence
D. compound-complex sentence

Answer: C and D

Explanation: A complex sentence combines a dependent clause with an independent clause. Subsequently, a compound-complex sentence requires a dependent clause.

QUESTION 41

cake – fake – make – bake – snake

The above words share all the following except?

A. rime
B. vowel
C. morpheme
D. long-vowel /e/ digraph

Answer: D

Explanation: All words contain morphemes. The words in the list rime and all have vowels. There is no indication of a long-vowel /e/ digraph in the words listed.

QUESTION 42

Which of the following versions of a sentence from a student's draft of an expository essay would be most effective for the student to use to convey an idea clearly and concisely?

  A. Blue birds are tiny and delicate. During migration, they can fly as far as 1000 miles one way.
  B. Blue birds are tiny, seemingly delicate creatures, but during migration they can fly as far as 1000 miles one way.
  C. Due to their tiny size, few would know that blue birds have the ability to fly as far as 1000 miles one way.
  D. Blue birds may be tiny but they have features that include migrating as far as 1000 miles one way.

Answer: B

Explanation: Option B does not include extra words and written in a concise and clear manner. Option A has two sentences, which is unnecessary. Options C and D are wordy compared to Option B.

QUESTION 43

Objective: The students are to write paragraph(s) that introduce an opinion, with concluding statements that explain why a certain action needs to be taken.

Which of the following activities would be most appropriate for the second-grade students to work on for the objective?

  A. read an opinion statement and summarize it
  B. write a letter to the principal in response to the new uniform policy
  C. write an essay on the impact of the American Revolution
  D. research a topic related to the best cooking show

Answer: B

Explanation: Option B allows the students to provide opinion related to the new uniform policy. Options C and D do not allow students to formulate opinions. In addition, Option A requires students to summarize opinion as opposed to formulate.

QUESTION 44

A sixth-grade teacher is looking to monitor students' progress related to explaining the relationship between few concepts in an informational text by drawing on precise information in the text. Which of the following types of assessments would be most beneficial for the teacher to use for this purpose?

A. open-ended questions that test students' ability on inferential comprehension related to information text

B. in-class discussions of key concepts followed by independent writing assignment involving citing details from text when making connection between concepts

C. in-class discussions of key concepts followed by group writing assignment involving citing details from text when making connection between concepts

D. open-ended questions that test students' ability on literal comprehension related to information text

Answer: B

Explanation: Option B allows the teacher to monitor students in group discussion, but also allows the teacher to see how students perform independently, which is the most beneficial for the teacher for assessment purposes.

QUESTION 45

Which factor contributes the most in reading comprehension acquisition among students in the first-grade?

A. concept of print

B. vocabulary development

C. decoding skills

D. oral language development

Answer: C

Explanation: Many factors can contribute in reading comprehension difficulty and acquisition for first-grade students. Much research suggests that lack of decoding skills contributes in reading comprehension difficulty for students in the first-grade.

QUESTION 46

Use the excerpt below from a small-group discussion to answer the question that follows.

> Student 1: Okay, let's work together to get this poster completed. We can all do
> something for the post. I think I will draw.
> Student 2: Do you mean draw the content or pictures, or both?
> Student 1: Just the pictures. Do you want to write the content?
> Student 3: I can help with the content. What are you going to draw?
> Student 2: I will help with the content too.
> Student 1: I will draw the cat and dog.

The excerpt best exemplifies which of the following forms of interpersonal communications?

    A. analyzing

    B. clarifying

    C. confirming

    D. completing

Answer: B

Explanation: The discussion shows that the students are asking clarification questions to know what to complete for the poster project.

QUESTION 47

> Martha really needed to get to the bus, so she ran like the wind.

The sentence above uses which of the following literary element?

    A. simile

    B. personification

    C. oxymoron

    D. hyperbole

Answer: A

Explanation: Simile is an expression comparing one thing to another using "like" or "as."

QUESTION 48

An elementary reading teacher is going to have her students read an informational text about the tropical rainforest. Prior to reading the informational text, the teacher is going to review academic vocabulary words. Why is it important to teach academic vocabulary to students at the elementary grade levels?

   A. Such vocabulary is very difficult to articulate.
   B. Such vocabulary relates to students who are visual.
   C. Such vocabulary is not typically used during informal conversation.
   D. Such vocabulary is completely unknown to students and using context clues to determine meaning is impossible.

Answer: C

Explanation: Academic language is words used in content areas and field-specific. The words are not used by elementary students daily. Therefore, a teacher has to plan to teach academic vocabulary to ensure better comprehension of text.

QUESTION 49

Kelly is willing to run in the hot sun, but Jack is <u>reluctant</u> and goes inside because of the hot temperatures.

Which type of context clue in the sentence helps decode the meaning of the underlined word?

   A. contrast
   B. furthermore
   C. example
   D. definition

Answer: A

Explanation: Kelly is willing to run in the hot sun, but Jake is reluctant to go in the hot sun. Jake's action is contrasted with that of Kelly's. Reluctant means "not willing."

QUESTION 50

A teacher is informally assessing third-grade students' listening comprehension skills after reading aloud the fable "The Rat and the Elephant." Which of the following prompts requires the students to draw an inference from the fable?

    A. Who are the characters in the fable?
    B. What is the rat used to?
    C. How does the cat demonstrate how the rat is not as impressive as the elephant?
    D. What lesson does the fable teach?

Answer: D

Explanation: An inference is a conclusion that is not clearly and directly stated in the reading. Only Option B requires the students to tell what the story teaches in their own words. This information is not clearly and directly stated in the text.

QUESTION 51

Month	Week 1	Week 2	Week 3
Child's spelling of "coat"	ct	cot	cote

Based on the information in the chart above, it can be inferred that the child is

    A. unaware of the relationship between letters and sounds.
    B. unaware of the concept of alphabetic principle.
    C. progressing related to the relationship between letters and sounds.
    D. progressing on the concept of alphabetic principle.

Answer: C

Explanation: The student attempts to spell "coat" over time showing a growing knowledge in phonics, in particular CVC words. The student starts off with spelling just the beginning and ending consonants. Then, later the student adds a vowel. Then, at the end, the student adds "e," which is incorrect, but still shows progression.

QUESTION 52

After reading a picture book regarding the different weather seasons with a class of kindergartners, a teacher talks about the seasons. Then, the teacher instructs the students to use the pictures in the book to talk about seasons with their peers. The teacher's approach best allows oral language development in young students by

    A. helping them understand their environment.
    B. promoting them to engage in conversation.
    C. using texts to relate to their personal lives.
    D. helping them think-aloud to encourage thought.

Answer: B

Explanation: The main purpose of the activity is to get the students to engage in conversation, which allows oral language development.

QUESTION 53

Students have written their first draft for the writing prompt provided by their teacher. Which of the following strategies would be the next most beneficial for the students?

    A. rereading independently the essay
    B. checking if ideas are correctly written
    C. holding peer conferences
    D. adding more details to paragraphs

Answer: C

Explanation: After the first draft, the next stage in the writing process is revising, which includes having others look at the essay. Option C is the most beneficial option.

QUESTION 54

Jimmy is a fifth-grade student, and his English teacher is going to have him present his research on bowling to his classmates. Jimmy is very shy and nervous about presenting in front of his classmates. To support Jimmy, which of the following is the most helpful?

    A. memorize everything for the presentation
    B. type everything that he will say in the presentation
    C. write keywords on note cards to use during presentation
    D. write vocabulary words he has difficulty understanding

Answer: C

Explanation: Writing keywords on note cards related to the presentation will support him to smoothly communicate his presentation to his classmates.

QUESTION 55

An elementary education teacher is having her students read Belling the Cat. After reading, the teacher has her students write a summary of the story. What is the primary purpose of this activity?

    A. to see if the students understand key vocabulary words
    B. to see if students comprehend the text
    C. to see if the students can write properly
    D. to see if the students have good fluency rate

Answer: B

Explanation: Having students write a summary of a story after reading the story shows the teacher is seeking to see if the students comprehend the text. Nothing suggests the purpose is related to vocabulary words, fluency, or writing.

QUESTION 56

Which of the following concepts involves understanding the letter-sound or sound-symbol relationships of language and helps readers to sound out unknown words?

- A. graphophonic cues
- B. morphology
- C. phonemic awareness
- D. syntax

Answer: A

Explanation: Graphophonic cues involve understanding the letter-sound or sound-symbol relationships of language and helps readers to sound out unknown words.

QUESTION 57

Which of the following is NOT an imperative sentence?

- A. Please pass the water.
- B. Don't write too much.
- C. I need to eat bread.
- D. Go to mom's house.

Answer: C

Explanation: Imperative sentences are used to issue a command or instruction, make a request, or offer advice.

QUESTION 58

Which of the following accurately describes footnotes or endnotes? Selection TWO answers.

    A. Footnotes appear at the bottom of each page they refer to.

    B. Footnotes appear at the very end of a text.

    C. Endnotes appear at the bottom of each page they refer to.

    D. Endnotes appear at the very end of a text.

Answer: A and D

Explanation: Footnotes appear at the bottom of each page they refer to while endnotes appear at the very end of a text.

QUESTION 59

Billy's dad, a farmer, owns a land in Texas. Which of the following resources is best for Billy's dad?

    A. dictionary

    B. atlas

    C. almanac

    D. thesaurus

Answer: C

Explanation: An almanac is an annual publication listing of a set of events forthcoming in the next year. It includes information like weather forecasts, farmers' planting dates, etc. Of the options, an almanac is the best use for a farmer.

QUESTION 60

The following is a selection from Alfred Noyes' poem "The Highwayman."

The wind was a torrent of darkness among the gusty trees.
The moon was a ghostly galleon tossed upon cloudy seas.
The road was a ribbon of moonlight over the purple moor,
And the highwayman came riding—
Riding—riding—
The highwayman came riding, up to the old inn-door.

He'd a French cocked-hat on his forehead, a bunch of lace at his chin,
A coat of the claret velvet, and breeches of brown doe-skin.
They fitted with never a wrinkle. His boots were up to the thigh.
And he rode with a jewelled twinkle,
His pistol butts a-twinkle,
His rapier hilt a-twinkle, under the jewelled sky.

What is the rhyme scheme for the above poem?

- A. aabccb
- B. ababab
- C. aaccbb
- D. aacbcb

Answer: A

Explanation: The rhyme scheme is aabccb:

> The wind was a torrent of darkness among the gusty trees, A
> The moon was a ghostly galleon tossed upon cloudy seas, A
> The road was a ribbon of moonlight over the purple moor, B
> And the highwayman came riding-- C
> Riding--riding-- C
> The highwayman came riding, up to the old inn-door. B

QUESTION 61

Which of the following require the need to cite reference material? Select TWO answers.

    A. using quotations

    B. paraphrasing

    C. documenting conversations

    D. stating facts

Answer: A and B

Explanation: Using quotes or paraphrasing involves using someone else is statements or ideas, which require writers to cite references.

QUESTION 62

Which of the following writing development phase is shown in the sample above?

    A. picture writing

    B. scribble writing

    C. random letter

    D. invented spelling

Answer: B

Explanation: Scribble writing is one of the first steps in learning to write, and the scribbles may not make any sense to an adult.

QUESTION 63

For a project regarding painting techniques of Vincent van Gogh for upper elementary students, which of the following is the most appropriate keyword to search when looking for resources on the internet or library catalog?

A. art
B. painting
C. techniques
D. Vincent van Gogh

Answer: D

Explanation: Options A, B, and C are too general words to use, but Option D is detailed to get good results.

QUESTION 64

Which of the following is the most effective way to develop decoding, fluency, vocabulary development, text comprehension, and learner engagement?

A. choral reading
B. round-robin reading
C. readers theatre
D. repeated reading

Answer: B

Explanation: The purpose of round-robin reading is to engage all learners. In this approach, each student reads small portion of the text aloud to the class and then a new reader is selected. This gives students opportunity for decoding, fluency, vocabulary development, text comprehension, and learner engagement.

QUESTION 65

A fourth-grade teacher asks the students to partner to read a literary selection. The teacher puts few questions on a worksheet for students to answer while reading the story. Which type of assessment is the teacher using?

    A. informal
    B. formal
    C. diagnostic
    D. standardized

Answer: B

Explanation: Since the teacher is using a worksheet that students will complete, the teacher is using a formal assessment. Formal assessments are preplanned tests that measure how well students have mastered learning outcomes.

QUESTION 66

Which of the following modes of writing is intended to provide a story about a friend's birthday party experience?

    A. descriptive
    B. narrative
    C. expository
    D. persuasive

Answer: B

Explanation: Narrative writing is fiction or non-fiction, and it tells others the stories of personal experiences. Writing a story about a friend's birthday party is narrative writing.

QUESTION 67

A first-grade teacher starts a reading activity by pointing out the title, author, illustrator, and title page. Which skill is this teacher most likely targeting?

    A. generating ideas

    B. expanding vocabulary

    C. concepts about words

    D. concepts about books

Answer: D

Explanation: Title, author, illustrator, and title page are all elements of books, so the teacher is targeting the concept of books.

QUESTION 68

Which of the following is the best demonstration of phonemic segmenting from first-grade students working with the word "bumping"?

    A. bump-ing

    B. bu-mp-ing

    C. bum-pi-ng

    D. b-u-m-p-i-n-g

Answer: D

Explanation: At first grade level, there is some competency shown in phonemic segmenting, so Option D is the best answer.

QUESTION 69

An elementary education student is interested in the following from a book:

- overview of text
- relationship among topics
- organization of the text

The best place for the student to look at in the text is which of the following?

A. footnotes
B. glossary
C. index
D. table of contents

Answer: D

Explanation: The table of content can provide information on overview of text, relationship between topics, and organization of topics.

QUESTION 70

In order to prepare students to read about different animals, the teacher organized a field trip to the local zoo and arranged a presentation by the zoo master for the class. The teacher is developing

A. background information and purpose.
B. interest and motivation.
C. oral language skills.
D. background information, presentation skills, and purpose.

Answer: A

Explanation: Prior to reading the text, the teacher is organizing a field trip to the zoo, which indicates the teacher wants the students to gain background knowledge and purpose regarding animals.

QUESTION 71

A third-grade teacher has been using a number of anecdotal records compiled over several months about a student. From the information, the teacher notes that the student is having trouble with pronouns and nouns agreement and develops a set of remediation activities for that student. Which of the following responses is an example of another qualitative measure to use for assessment purposes?

    A. summative assessments

    B. diagnostic assessments

    C. equitable assessments

    D. portfolio assessments

Answer: D

Explanation: Anecdotal records are detailed, narrative descriptions of an incident involving one or several children, which can be useful details. To provide another reliable qualitative measure, portfolio assessments are the best. The portfolio assessments allows examining various sample documents to see progression.

QUESTION 72

    -   coming ready for discussion

    -   staying on topic

    -   maintaining eye-contact

The above best supports students in

    A. ensuring the audience's comprehension.

    B. getting to learn more about audience.

    C. helping sell the topic.

    D. speaking better

Answer: A

Explanation: When presenting, performers need to focus on ensuring that the audience can comprehend the message, which include coming ready for discussion, staying on topic, and maintaining eye-contact.

QUESTION 73

_____ are objects and materials from everyday life, especially when used as teaching aids.

A. Modeling
B. Dictation
C. Realia
D. Role playing

Answer: C

Explanation: Realia are objects and materials from everyday life, especially when used as teaching aids.

QUESTION 74

Teacher: What is the first sound in ban?

Student: The first sound is /b/.

The above represents which of the following phonemic-awareness strategies?

A. isolation
B. categorization
C. blending
D. segmentation

Answer: A

Explanation: Phoneme isolation is the ability to identify where a sound appears in a word or to identify what sound appears in a given position in a word.

QUESTION 75

do – said – was – of

The above list best represent which of the following?

    A. regular words

    B. passive words

    C. irregular words

    D. active words

Answer: C

Explanation: Irregular words cannot be decoded.

QUESTION 76

In a kindergarten class, the teacher reads "Playing with Friends" aloud, while the students echo the words the teacher has read. Which of the following approaches to reading is being undertaken in this activity?

    A. guided reading

    B. shared reading

    C. active reading

    D. round robin

Answer: B

Explanation: Shared reading is an interactive reading experience in which students join in the reading of a big book or other enlarged text as guided by a teacher.

QUESTION 77

The following is an excerpt from second-grade student's work.

Betty and her friend are going to play, so there are not board. There are excited about the fun day. There have a good planned out day.

The above sentence shows that the student needs help in which of the following?

A. homophones
B. phonics
C. antonyms
D. synonyms

Answer: A

Explanation: The student made several homophone errors, included confusing "bored" with "board" and "their" with "there."

QUESTION 78

Which of the following spelling patterns is found in the word "poke"?

A. CV
B. CVC
C. CVCe
D. CVVC

Answer: C

Explanation: The CVCe pattern includes words that have an "e" at the end of the word, which typically makes the vowel of the word sound long.

QUESTION 79

The following is a writing piece from a student's journal:

We had a good vacation. We went in the car for the trip. We saw many nice buildings.

To help the student improve the writing piece, what instructional strategy is the best?

A. explain the concept of using various types of sentences
B. ask questions about the vacation
C. show student examples of good and concise sentences
D. ask questions about the car

Answer: B

Explanation: More details are needed in the writing piece. By asking questions to the student, the approach will trigger the student to provide more details.

QUESTION 80

Which of the following diagrams can not be used to assist students in identifying main ideas?

A.

B.

C.

D.

Answer: D

Explanation: The hamburger method is used in writing to construct body paragraphs (topic sentence, detail sentences, and concluding sentences). All other options allow the students to document details and write main idea.

PRAXIS 5002 Reading and Language Arts Elementary Education

By: LQ Publications

This page is intentionally left blank.

CPSIA information can be obtained
at www.ICGtesting.com
Printed in the USA
BVHW010210290621
610716BV00012B/377